WHY

CUSTOMERS

COME BACK

How to Create
Lasting Customer Loyalty

Manzie R. Lawfer

CAREER
PRESS
Franklin Lakes, NJ

WHY CUSTOMERS COME BACK
EDITED AND TYPESET BY KRISTEN PARKES
Cover design by Cheryl Cohan Finbow
Printed in the U.S.A. by Book-mart Press

To order this title, please call toll-free 1-800-CAREER-1 (NJ and Canada: 201-848-0310) to order using VISA or MasterCard, or for further information on books from Career Press.

The Career Press, Inc., 3 Tice Road, PO Box 687,
Franklin Lakes, NJ 07417
www.careerpress.com

Library of Congress Cataloging-in-Publication Data

Lawfer, Manzie R., 1946-
  Why customers come back : how to create lasting customer loyalty /
Manzie R. Lawfer.
    p. cm.
  Includes index.
  ISBN 1-56414-695-2 (pbk.)
    1. Customer loyalty. 2. Customer relations. I. Title.

HF5415.525.L39 2004
658.8'343—dc21

                                                        2003054650

Dedication

This book is dedicated to my parents,
Larry and Rena Lawfer, who were persistent in
their encouragement long before I ever wrote
my first word.

Acknowledgments

I would like to acknowledge and thank the many business owners, executives, captains of industry, and consumers that have been so generous with their honesty and time in helping me research this book.

My literary agent, Wendy Keller, of ForthWrite Literary Agency and Speakers Bureau, has been, and continues to be, a source of concern, care, encouragement, friendship, and guidance, which have been priceless. If you are looking for an agent, look no further.

I especially want to acknowledge and thank my wife, JoyAnn, for her loyalty and willingness to allow me to move writing from my avocation to my profession.

Contents

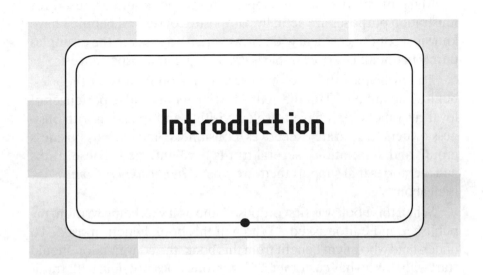

Introduction

Welcome to *Why Customers Come Back*. This book might have been titled *What You Can Do to Get Your Customers to Come Back* because what I have written about is what motivates customers to do business with you and how you can use this information to develop a customer base that returns to do business with you again and again.

During the past nearly 30 years, I have studied and learned about customers and their buying habits and experiences. What has evolved from this study is the understanding that five principles determine customer loyalty. I did not invent these principles; however, I did discover them and put them into a concise and learnable form. These principles were scattered in hundreds of books and articles. They were discussed in hundreds, perhaps thousands, of interviews with consumers, captains of industry, and business leaders. Each source knew this small piece or that tiny part, but no one source was familiar with all five principles. I have learned that any one of the five principles will increase loyalty, but when all five principles are put to use, the results are astounding. My intent in writing this book is to share what I have learned from my research.

Many of the people who appear in this book and are used for illustration purposes are actually composites of several people I have known or continue to deal with. However, in no case are the examples purely fictional: Every example is grounded in real experiences.

The principles that are discussed in this book are not theories, but instead are based on the actual buying habits and experiences of loyal customers. As I have traveled, visiting and speaking with business owners, corporate executives, consumers, and various business groups and associations, several truths have emerged. These truths and the stories that support them are what *Why Customers Come Back* is all about.

When this book was first proposed and as it was being written, my publisher and editor asked, "Who will this book benefit most?" To understand who might benefit from this book, the conversation should start with, "Who has customers?" Everyone does not deal with traditional external customers, but all of us do have internal customers. The principles that create customer loyalty apply to all customers. The answer, then, is that we all have customers and the principles that create loyalty apply equally to both internal and external customers. However, please note this book is not a compilation of sales techniques. In fact, this book will not help salespeople prospect, close sales, or do any of the things that traditional sales books describe. This book is about a larger relationship between you and your customers.

Many businesses display banners proclaiming, "Build Customer Loyalty!" but offer no training or tools to accomplish that mission. This is the moral equivalent of an athletic coach cupping his hands around his mouth and yelling at his players, "Score more points!" Scoring more points is no more intuitive than building customer loyalty. "More points" and "customer loyalty" are outcomes that occur because the participants are executing specific and certain activities that promote the results. The exhortation is meaningless without knowledge of the activity that will produce the result.

Why Customers Come Back is not about yelling, "Build Customer Loyalty!" This book is about discovering the motivation and characteristics of loyal customers, the advantages of dealing with loyal customers, and most importantly, what each of us can do to create loyalty with our customers.

Companies tend to ask the question, "Which of our customers are most loyal?" I see hundreds of Websites, consulting services, and books that want to help businesses by determining who their loyal customers might be. The whole exercise revolves around identifying specific customers or groups of customers. This thinking ultimately blames customers for their disloyalty or believes loyalty to be a characteristic of only some customers. Further, the act of identifying loyal customers only identifies them as loyal and doesn't reveal *why* they are loyal.

Customers have no interest whatsoever in loyalty. They only buy products and services that satisfy their own needs. Customer loyalty is a response to how a business presents its products and services. The only reason anyone buys anything is because they want to buy it. No one has an obligation to continue buying from any business. Your customers continue to buy from you because of the relationship you have with them of offering your products and services in a way that appeals to them.

Is the customer to blame when a company fails to provide products and services in an appealing manner? Does it make sense to call a customer disloyal because a company is not doing the things that appeal to the customer and they shop someplace else? When competition offers better products, lower prices, or some other advantage, should your customer continue doing business with you?

Customers are self-serving: Their only interest is to deal with a business that gives them what they want. Customers are not inherently loyal or disloyal; loyalty is not a characteristic of customers, it is a customer's response to the actions of you and your business.

The question should never be, "Which of our customers are most loyal?" or "Why aren't our customers more loyal?" The question should always be, "What can we do to make the customer want to come back?" The issue of customer loyalty is central to the business, not to the customer.

This book is about working with current customers to develop lasting loyalty. I believe that the concepts and stories presented here will benefit everyone who has customers. No business is exempt from the benefit of dealing with loyal customers.

As I write these words, it is October 2003. The U.S. economy has been slow to rebound, and while there have been positive signs of growth, many businesses and professionals continue to suffer with lackluster performance and reduced profits.

Customer loyalty is the answer today as it has been in the past and will be in the future. Loyal customers are easier to do business with, are more predictable, and don't carry the expense associated with attracting new customers. Companies with a loyal customer base enjoy greater profitability in good economic times and depend on their loyal customers to help them survive difficult financial conditions.

American businesses typically attempt to create loyalty through customer satisfaction and special incentives. The satisfaction movement began 20 years ago with the release of Tom Peters' classic book *In Search of Excellence*. The book spawned hundreds of copycat books and seminars, but despite all the effort to increase customer satisfaction, disciples of the customer satisfaction movement don't see any more customer loyalty today then they did 20 years ago. This book answers the question, "If satisfaction doesn't create loyal customers, what does?"

I hope you enjoy this book, but more importantly, I hope you put into practice the principles that create customer loyalty. Creating customer loyalty is the single most important and beneficial endeavor for every business.

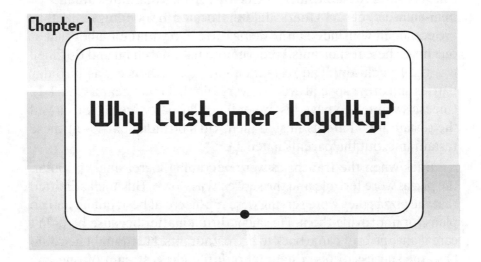

Chapter 1

Why Customer Loyalty?

American business can be fickle. People change their preferences. People change their minds. Technology, the Internet, and overnight delivery to anywhere in the country has changed the rules of competition. Mom-and-pop corner stores must now compete with businesses a thousand miles away.

Getting customers to come back again and again is the most important endeavor of every business. No business can be successful by continually dealing with new customers. Repeat customers are the source of all profit, and profit allows a business to grow and prosper.

Chuck E. Cheese's Learns the Value of Repeat Customers

In 1977, Nolan Bushnell, the inventor and founder of the Atari video game company sold his company for a fortune. Bushnell opened a new business called Chuck E. Cheese's. The restaurants are indoor mini-amusement parks that sell pizza. Located in shopping malls, they are equipped with video and other games. Do you remember that at one time, these restaurants were part of a national chain and Bushnell was the franchiser? The restaurant's target audience was birthday parties and other special events. Every kid that lived near a Chuck E. Cheese's wanted to have his or her birthday party there: Kids loved the restaurants. Parents hosted their kid's birthday parties at these restaurants, but the parents hated it.

Back when the franchises were becoming increasingly popular, the pizzas were terrible and the service was worse. Bushnell admitted that the pizzas they were serving were mediocre at best, but he had no plans for improving them. He said it didn't matter because he didn't care if anyone ever came back to his restaurants. He thought he could base the success of his restaurant on an endless stream of onetime customers. His plan was flawed because word of poor service and terrible pizza traveled quickly. Despite the pleas from their children parents refused to be subjected to Chuck E. Cheese's.

Instead of an endless stream of new customers, every customer that visited Chuck E. Cheese's told others about their terrible experience. Bushnell's dream collapsed shortly after it began: Negative word-of-mouth advertising ended his ability to franchise these restaurants.

Every business depends on loyal customers coming back again and again. Some of Chuck E. Cheese's franchisees continued their operations, independent of Bushnell, with a philosophy of building a repeat customer trade. Many of these businesses have prospered by depending on loyal customers. Businesses cannot prosper or even exist without repeat customers. The Chuck E. Cheese's establishments that adapted and made a commitment to repeat business are thriving today. Today, kids love having their birthday party at a Chuck E. Cheese's and their parents love it, too.

The value of customer loyalty is not situational or temporary. Loyal customers are always valuable. Customer loyalty is never the problem; it is always the solution. Customer loyalty levels the playing field; it is the ultimate competitive advantage.

Customer loyalty is an activity; it is not an emotion or an opinion. When customers buy from you again and again and tell the world why everyone else should buy from you, they are demonstrating loyalty. Customer loyalty is the specific activity of buying from you or recommending you to others on a repeat basis.

Customer Loyalty Is Not an Opinion

When I was a kid growing up in a small Alabama town, there was a little grocery store that was the only place to shop. Horace's wasn't much bigger than a modern convenience store, but it was the only grocery store within 15 miles of our town. Most everyone in our community did their shopping at Horace's. I do not remember anyone ever saying that Horace's had the best prices, selection, service, or the best of anything; simply, people shopped there because it was closest. If someone was passing through town and asked where a grocery store was, the answer had to be Horace's. If nothing else, Horace's had a loyal clientele because the same people came back every week. The family that owned Horace's enjoyed all the benefits of loyal customers. The family made a fortune because they were the only store in town.

When suburbanization brought a real supermarket to our town, the community suddenly had a choice of where to shop. The new supermarket was much larger, cleaner, and had more selection. Horace's was forced to either adapt or die. Horace's had never done anything to create loyalty except be the only grocery store in town.

Before the new supermarket moved in, the people of our town were demonstrating loyalty by shopping at Horace's every week. Their opinion of Horace's didn't make one whit of difference. The shoppers voted with their pocketbooks and the owners counted their votes in the store's cash register.

Horace's owners might have been able to do a lot of things to compete with the supermarket chain store, but they only did what they had always done. Over a relatively short period of time, the people of our town began doing most of their shopping at the new supermarket.

Horace's still had a good location, but the owners went from making a fortune to making a living. The people of our town still had a good opinion of Horace's, but given a choice, they preferred to shop elsewhere. Loyalty is not an emotion or an opinion, it is only an activity.

All Profit Comes From Loyal Customers

Repeat customers are the only source of profit for any business. It is not until a customer buys from you a second, third, or fourth time that any profit is earned. The cost of attracting and learning how to serve first-time customers consumes any potential profit that might be made.

Modern accounting methods are very precise in the measurement of costs, expenses, worth of inventory, and the relationships of these values. However, modern accounting methods are nearly worthless when it comes to measuring the value of customers and their relative loyalty. Your accountant or accounting department can tell you to the penny how much profit you made last year. Unfortunately, accounting principles do not reveal and, in fact, hide which customers produced the profit.

For example, I shop for office supplies at Office Depot. They have a great selection, good prices, and their store is close to my home-office. Office Depot advertises on television and in the newspaper and offers their products for sale on the Internet. They also send advertisements through the mail and have a display rack in the front of their store with flyers that describe their current specials. The Office Depot at which I shop is open from 8 a.m. till 9 p.m. The store is well staffed with bright and helpful employees.

As a writer, I use a lot of printer cartridges, paper, and other office supplies. When I visit Office Depot, I do not need an employee to help me find what I'm going to buy because I am already familiar with the location of the supplies I need. I usually shop mid-morning during the week, so its extended hours during the week and weekend hours of operation are of no interest to me. I pay for my purchases with cash, so I do not use the credit terms they offer. I am pleased with Office Depot and visit the store regularly. Its advertisements, special offers, and Internet store are enticements that do not really apply to me. I am a loyal customer of Office Depot but I use very few of the added benefits they provide.

When Office Depot's executives report to their stockholders through their annual report, I am not mentioned. The few thousand dollars I spend with the company each year are mixed in with the rest of the $11 billion in revenue. The executives and stockholders cannot see that most of their expenses in additional hours, advertising, Website maintenance, and employee training are wasted on me. If all of Office Depot's customers were like me, it could save a fortune. I'm not a big customer for Office Depot, but on the basis of an expense to revenue ratio, percentage-wise, I'm a very profitable customer for this company. Modern accounting methods will never disclose this profitability. All of Office Depot's customers, just like everybody else's customers, must share the burden of the company's total expenses.

All of this is to say that modern accounting methods do not fairly describe the true profitability from a loyal repeat customer. However, Frederick F. Reichheld, loyalty expert and author of *The Loyalty Effect*, reports that even a marginal increase of just 5 percent repeat business produces a whopping 60-percent increase in profit.

When your customers come back to buy from you a second, third, or fourth time, they already know where you are located and what service and products your business provides. You don't have to educate these people about your business because they already know, so you do not have the expense of advertising in order to attract them. These repeat customers are easier to do business with because of what you know about each other. Time and money are saved and you earn a profit where profit did not previously exist.

The Value of Predictability

We saw how Horace's inability to adapt was its downfall. Adaptability is important, even critical, to our continued success, but we also must be able to predict the behavior of our customers. Predictability is an important benefit of having loyal customers. Predictability allows a business to maximize its resources today and plan for the future. When you can predict your customers' buying habits, you are also able to predict staffing, inventory, and every other aspect of your business.

Do you like hot dogs?

Dean was let go from his corporate position with Sears when the company was going through one of its many downsizing efforts. As a result, he bought a fairly elaborate and sophisticated hot dog cart and began an entrepreneurial adventure that far surpassed his fondest expectations. No one wants to be fired from their job, but Dean took it in stride and said he looked forward to being his own boss even if it was only as a hot dog vendor.

Dean towed the sophisticated hot dog cart behind his car to a spot in front of the courthouse every day it was not raining or too cold. On the way he stopped to buy hot dogs, buns, and other supplies. When he first started his business, he usually bought too many hot dogs. On a good day he would sell 50 to 60 hot dogs and would have to throw away as many as 20 to 30 hot dogs and buns. Dean only wanted to offer the freshest product and refused to sell hot dogs that were a day old. You don't need to do the math to understand his problem. He was buying too many hot dogs for the amount of customers he had. His inventory costs included the price of 90 hot dogs and buns, but he only had the revenue from the sale of 50 or 60 hot dogs. He was spending too much for inventory, but on the other hand, he didn't want to run out of hot dogs to sell. Dean thought that if he turned a customer away because he was out of hot dogs the customer might never come back again.

Fortunately, Dean very quickly began to predict his inventory needs by noting how many customers he had each day. Not only did this predictability allow him to regulate his inventory, he also was able to determine his most productive sales hours. He refined his calculations for time of year and weather conditions. Pretty soon Dean could predict within three to five hot dogs exactly how many hot dogs he would sell on a given Monday, Tuesday, Wednesday, Thursday, or Friday. Because Dean had developed a loyal (predictable) customer base, he purchased almost the exact amount of product he would sell and he knew which were his best hours of operation. His inventory cost became a much smaller amount in relation to his sales. Dean had very little wasted product, and so his profits doubled. Not only did his profits double, but he was working fewer hours because he knew when his loyal customers would show up hungry.

It is interesting to note that in his first year of business, Dean was earning more money selling hot dogs than he ever did working in corporate America.

Dean's hot dog stand is a simple business model but it makes the point that the predictability that comes from repeat purchasing by your customers will substantially increase your profit, as well as reduce the time it takes to make it.

The Price of Attraction

Predictability is only one advantage to having loyal customers. The cost to attract a new customer is a large expense that is affected by customer loyalty. General Motors recently disclosed that it spends as much as $2,500 to attract each new customer. All of its customers are not new, but General Motors spends considerable sums of time and money trying to attract more than 20 percent new customers each year. The $2,500 General Motors spends on each of these new customers cancels out every penny of potential profit.

The average price of a new General Motors automobile is approximately $20,000. According to its annual reports, GM's earnings are traditionally less than 10 percent of its revenue. Ten percent of $20,000 (its average-priced automobile) is $2,000. That means its average profit per automobile is $2,000, while its average cost to attract a new customer is $2,500. General Motors spends $500 more to attract each new customer than it can hope to make. In order for General Motors to make any profit from these people, it has to sell them a second, third, or fourth automobile.

Advertising, signs, promotions, and special sales are just a few of the additional expenses of attracting new customers. If you consider all of your expenses in trying to attract new customers you'll discover that you are not making any profit from new customers on their first purchase. As with General Motor's customer, your customer has to come back a second or third time for you to make a profit.

The cost to attract one new customer

The customers you have today know your business: They know your location, your selection, and how you do business. You may want to advertise to your current customers to inform them of a sale or special promotion, but generally your current customers already know all about you. How much does it cost to attract new customers that don't know about you?

You don't need a billboard to attract your loyal customers

Johnny's Steak House is a terrific restaurant located in northern California. The restaurant is situated not far from Interstate 5, but you can't see it from the highway. This restaurant has enjoyed a loyal clientele of local folks for many years. Recently, a large billboard sign was erected on the Interstate that posts directions to Johnny's Steak House. The billboard sign costs the restaurant's owner $1,000 a month to rent. When a new customer sees the sign and comes into Johnny's, the owner doesn't make a profit. He doesn't make a profit until enough new customers come in each month to pay for the sign. He didn't need the sign for his regular customers because they already know that Johnny's is a terrific steak house and they know where it is located. The sign is only needed to attract new customers.

Once someone has been to Johnny's they know where it is, so the directions on the billboard are no longer necessary for them. When new customers come back a second, third, or fourth time, the restaurant makes a profit. There is no cost, or at most a reduced cost, to attract repeat customers; consequently, they are the only source of profit for a business.

The Ease of Doing Business

Predictability and a reduction in costs to attract new customers are not the only advantages to having loyal customers. There is a third advantage that helps reduce cost in dealing with customers. New customers have to learn how to buy from you, and teaching them takes time. You have to learn how to service new customers, and learning takes time. New customers may have bad credit habits, high returns, and a million other problems that need to be overcome before you can figure out how to best work with them, and overcoming these problems takes time. You must learn how (and if) these new customers are going to pay. You must learn what their delivery requirements might be. What styles or selection will these new customers prefer? Will these new customers be returning products or changing their minds on a regular basis? How demanding are they of service? How responsive are these new customers to special sales or promotions?

Only after you learn about them will you be able to deal with these new customers effectively. All this extra time costs you money—time is money—and all your potential profit is spent on learning how to deal with these new customers.

Renewing a Lease Is Easier

Charlie is a retired real estate agent in southwest Florida who owns several condominium units that he rents on an annual basis. When Charlie has a vacancy in one of his units, he places an advertisement in the local newspaper. He screens phone conversations with potential renters and only shows his property to those he thinks will be good tenants. When he shows the property, he completes a credit application and tries to learn as much about his prospective renter as possible.

Charlie and his wife spend their summers in the cool mountains of Tennessee. He does not want to have problems with property damage or rent collection during the summer when he is a thousand miles away from his property. Because Charlie knows he will be away from his rental property for several months, the amount of time and effort he spends screening and qualifying prospective tenants is substantial.

The amount of time Charlie spends renewing leasing with existing tenants is minimal. He knows his tenants: He has already transacted business with his existing tenant and he already knows what kind of tenant they are and if they are credit-worthy. Charlie understands the value of ease of doing business with a loyal tenant: Finding a new tenant is expensive and time-consuming, but renewing a lease is quick and easy.

Here's the good news: After you figure out how to deal with a new customer, you do not have to spend a great deal of money trying to attract the new customer, you have some level of predictability in dealing with the new customer, and you have an excellent chance to see some profit if they return to buy from you again.

Word-of-Mouth Marketing

Attracting and learning how to serve new customers can cost a substantial amount of money and can be very time consuming. Your loyal customers want to do this work for you at no charge. Loyal customers want to tell the whole world why everyone should buy from you, and they do not want a single penny for their effort.

When your customer tells her family and friends why they should buy from you, she is your advocate. Everyone likes a good deal. A good deal might be a better price, a special selection, or any number of other things. When your advocate tells someone else about you, she demonstrates that she feels good about her own purchase. She believes that you are the best at what you do, and that's why she wants to tell her friends and family about you. As an advocate, she gets to be a hero to her friends and family.

Remember when you had an especially good dinner in a new restaurant or a trouble-free auto repair experience? You couldn't wait to tell your friends about it. The restaurant and auto repair shop had no advertising cost because you were their advocate. This word-of-mouth advertising is the most effective way to attract new customers. Not only is it free, but your advocates have more credibility with their friends and family than you do. Because their recommendation is more credible, it is more valuable than any advertisement you could possibly buy.

Your advocate's recommendation affects the size and quality of business from the referred customer. The new customers that are referred to you will take less time to service, and in many cases, spend more money with you than your advocate spent. These new customers have been coached on your product or service and why it is the best. They will more readily make buying decisions because of this praise and coaching.

Building a Business on Word-of-Mouth Advertising

My friend, Larry Fisher graduated from Indiana University with a degree in marketing. His first job out of college was with Ashland Oil Company. Larry's job was to call on independent gas station owners to encourage them to sell more of Ashland's products.

Larry genuinely liked the people he called on. He developed strong business and personal relationships with these station owners. After a few years, Larry left his employment with Ashland and opened an insurance agency with the idea of providing gas station owners with property and casualty insurance.

While he doesn't turn other business away, Larry specializes in the gas station market. Larry relies on his knowledge of the oil industry and the network of gas station owners he knows. Customers are happy to refer Larry to other gas station owners because they believe he is the best at what he does. These gas station owners are Larry's advocates, and they make his advertising expense nearly nonexistent. He attends the annual gas dealer convention in his area but does not do any other form of advertising; all of his advertising comes from word-of-mouth. When a new gas station is being built, Larry's clients are quick to call him and let him know about the new station. Larry usually knows about new stations or the sale of existing stations long before his competitors. In his 25 years of business, he has lost very few clients and every year his agency has grown steadily. He provides insurance to more than 1,000 independent gas station owners.

At various times over the years, insurance companies Larry represents have decided to stop selling insurance to gas stations because of negative claims experience or perhaps a change in their marketing plans. The first time this happened Larry was quite concerned, but he was able to find another insurance carrier to replace the one leaving the marketplace.

When he told his clients about the new carrier, all of them bought insurance from the new company through Larry's agency: Larry's customers were loyal to him. The insurance carrier was not important to them; they simply wanted to continue to deal with Larry.

Larry is enjoying the benefits of having loyal repeat customers: Larry knows his customers because they are predictable, and he knows how to effectively and efficiently serve them. Larry's customers know him and know how to effectively and efficiently do business with him. This predictability lets Larry schedule with greater ease. Larry's customers do most of his prospecting for him, which saves him time and money. Larry enjoys the benefits and additional profits that come from having a loyal clientele. Larry's net profit is substantially greater than that of a similar sized agencies.

News articles scream, "America's business people need ways to increase profit and improve their image and standing with customers."

The dot-com fallout and credibility collapse of many major corporations has consumers retreating. Business people, entrepreneurs, corporate leaders and frontline employees who master the principles that create customer loyalty restore confidence and enjoy greater profit and the esteem of their customers.

The fiscal year 2002 was very difficult for the Ford Motor Company. The company suffered a $5 billion loss. It is difficult at best to understand automobile manufacturers' accounting. Carry forward losses, onetime accounting corrections, and many other factors go into determining paper profit and loss. However, no matter the strategy, Ford and its stockholders would have preferred a $5 billion profit. Over the years, Ford, similar to most other U.S. businesses, has focused on quality, price, market share, and a host of other business initiatives that have come and gone. For the year 2004, Ford has announced style and technology as cornerstones to turning their fortune around.

Toyota Motor Corporation had a terrific fiscal year 2002. The company had a net profit of $5 billion. Toyota's stockholders were thrilled with the company's performance. Toyota has built the company on the premise that all profit comes from loyal customers. It aggressively pursues loyalty. Toyota customers respond with fervent repeat buying. More than 70 percent of Toyota's customers return to buy another Toyota automobile. This is particularly remarkable when you consider that most automakers have only a 30-percent repeat purchase rate. Toyota focuses on its existing customers. Take a look at Toyota's brochures and other sales literature; typically, you will find an older model Toyota somewhere in the brochure. Toyota is saying, "It doesn't matter if the car is old or one of the new models, if you own one of our cars, you are part of the family."

Companies that promote and enjoy customer loyalty are more stable than companies that are forever searching for new markets and customers. A measure of this stability is the relative change in stock value. This change is calculated by using the selling value of a company's stock at the beginning of the year. Movement or change in the price of stock, either up or down, is totaled and divided by the opening price of the stock to calculate the percentage of change.

The Ford Motor Company aggressively pursues the attention of Wall Street investors and had a 94-percent swing in their stock value in fiscal 2002. Toyota Motor Corporation aggressively pursues customer loyalty and experienced a minimal stock value swing of only 36 percent during the same period. This change in stock price is even more astounding considering the huge stock market shifts that took place during this same period. Toyota's premise that all profit comes from loyal customers has provided stability and served their investors well.

Don't Shout Exhortations

Cheerleading and exhortations will not build loyalty. Why? Because loyalty is a behavior, an activity, and it will not be earned by simply telling customers what to do. The activity of repeat buying is a response to the five principles that create customer loyalty.

Remember Horace's Supermarket? The relationship its customers had with the store was based on one thing: it was the only grocery store for miles. It was a one-dimensional relationship built on being the only store around. As soon as the new supermarket moved into the area, customers began to build relationships based on service, selection, price, and convenience. All of us have seen this scenario played out again and again as stores such as Home Depot and Wal-Mart have moved into communities throughout the country. Yet despite the seemingly unfair advantage these major competitors have, many small local businesses have competed favorably. Invariably, the smaller businesses that continue to prosper have aggressively developed a loyalty relationship with their customers. You can also compete and prosper by learning and mastering the five principles that create loyalty and the activities that support them.

How We Learn

There are only four ways a person can learn. First, you can learn from your own mistakes, which is the most costly way to learn. Mistakes always cost time, money, or both. Second, you can learn from other people's mistakes, which is costly for the fellow that is providing the example. Third, you can learn from you own positive actions.

This method is not costly but may take several years. The fourth way you can learn is from the positive actions of others, which is the method best for all concerned. By learning from the successes of others you will learn without the pain or cost of mistakes and you will learn more quickly.

Sometimes it is difficult to resist telling stories about what goes wrong. Occasionally in this book, I do just that. Most of the time, however, this is a book about successfully developing loyal customers by learning how other people have done it. The five principles that create customer loyalty should sound familiar to you. They should resonate with you as we discuss each one and look at examples of how other people have put these principles into action. Each one of the principles will increase loyalty in your customers. As you master all five principles you will experience remarkable results.

In the next chapter you will learn that every business and every business model can benefit from having loyal customers. No business is exempt from the benefits or the ability to create loyalty.

Loyalty Creates Money

Customer loyalty creates money. We usually think of business endeavors in the same way we think of an athletic event: One team wins and the other team loses. One team gets the trophy or the prize and the losing team gets nothing.

In commerce we think of one business as getting the sale or the contract and the losing business as getting nothing. If one wins, then the other one must lose. This is not true when you consider customer loyalty. In the game of customer loyalty, when one business gains a loyal customer it is at no expense to the other company. Remember, the only time you can make a profit is when the customer returns to buy from you a second, third, or fourth time. If a customer is always buying from different businesses, there is no loyalty. No one is benefiting from repeat buying by making a profit from the customer. The customer is forever a new customer as he changes from one business to another. The customer doesn't even win, because he is not getting enough satisfaction out of any transaction or relationship to come back to buy from that business again.

However, when a company learns to give a customer what he wants, the customer becomes loyal. He buys on a repeat basis and creates profit where no profit existed before. This profit is not at the expense of the competition; it comes from the savings and other benefits derived from selling to a loyal customer—everyone wins. The competition is no longer losing money on the unfaithful customer. The business that has the customer's loyalty is now making a profit, which did not exist before. The customer is pleased enough with the transaction, relationship, products, or services to become a loyal customer. And that loyalty creates money.

The five principles that create customer loyalty are:

1. People do business with people.
2. Differentiation.
3. Value and assurance.
4. Effective communication.
5. Focus.

We will examine each of these five principles separately in the following chapters. You will learn that each of these principles can immediately affect your business; however, the most dramatic impact will come when you use all the principles together.

The five principles that create customer loyalty are supported by interpersonal skills. I don't want to spoil all the surprises that lie ahead for you in Chapter 3, but "people do business with people" is a self-descriptive phrase. People doing business with people is an interpersonal transaction. You will not have to become a psychologist to master this principle; however, you *will* benefit from remembering how this principle can be used to increase loyalty in your clientele. Each of the principles offers the opportunity to increase loyalty. A novice or the most experienced business leader can master each of the principles: No one is exempt from the benefits of creating loyalty and no one is exempt from the mastery of these principles. It is the choice of every business whether or not to create customer loyalty.

Destinations versus Journeys

I remember talking with a friend nearly 30 years ago shortly after we both had graduated from the University of Kentucky. We were both just starting our careers in business, and we were writing down our goals for the upcoming year. Our list of goals included all areas of our lives: health, wealth, spirituality, and happiness.

As we compared our goals for newer automobiles, better physical conditioning, owning our own homes, and all the other things we were dreaming of, my friend said, "If we want all this stuff so bad, why don't we already have it? If good physical conditioning is such a big deal, why aren't we already in tip-top physical condition? If being in great shape was a real priority for us, wouldn't we already be exercising every day?"

My friend was making the point that goals are destinations, but our lives are about journeys. Goals come and go, but the journey continues. The goals we set and accomplish for ourselves are mile markers on the journey of our lives. The goals we set for ourselves sometimes motivate and inspire us but it is our daily activities that are the real fabric of our lives.

Learning Which Is Which

Bernie and Leni Sweet are very creative and successful franchisees of several Arby's roast beef sandwich stores. Many of their employees are students and part-time workers new to the workforce. Leni teaches her employees that a clean store is not a destination, it is a journey. Keeping the dining room, kitchen, and bathrooms clean is an ongoing process. They are never finished with the job of cleaning. The good job they do at presenting a clean restaurant attracts customers and keeps them coming back. The more customers they have coming through the restaurant, the more it needs to be cleaned. Cleaning is not a destination, it is a journey.

Management

Many businesses manage by objective. Management by objective is when management describes the goal rather than the process. For example, the boss says, "You have to produce 200 widgets by this afternoon." As another example, the sales manager says, "You have to meet your third-quarter quota or we will be having a difficult conversation." This example is actually a "management by objective" statement with a threat thrown in to make sure you understand it is all about the numbers or the goal.

A difficulty with management by objective is that the objective is continually changing. The objective is a goal; it is not a process. Companies are forever changing their objective. This quarter the company is focused on getting new customers. Next quarter the company will be focused on revenue or cost-cutting measures. The objective and management of the objective are moving targets.

Management by Activity

When companies and individuals manage by activities there is a constancy of purpose. Activities can be monitored, refined, and adapted, but they are a permanent method of accomplishment. Objectives such as goals are temporary. An objective or goal is accomplished and then a new goal or objective replaces the old goal. For example, a company has a goal of reaching $100 million in sales this year. Every executive, manager, salesperson, and production worker is charged with doing his or her part in attaining the goal. If they attain their goal, next year you can bet the goal isn't going to be $100 million, it is going to be a larger number or there will be a new goal based on market share or some other qualifier.

Management by activity is continuous in nature. When a company manages by activity it is committing to constant improvement. Instead of asking the question, "How can we generate $100 million this year?" management by activity asks the questions, "How can we be more productive? How can we do our jobs better? How can we improve?"

Do You Have Children?

If you have young children, you probably know the challenges of having your kids keep their rooms clean. You might say, "This room is a wreck. I'll be back in 30 minutes and it better be clean." When you return in 30 minutes, little Henry is still sitting in the middle of the room playing with his toy cars surrounded by dirty laundry and toys. What happened? This is a classic example of management by objective. You told the little fellow what you wanted and not what he needed to do. You described the goal: a clean room. However, you did not describe the process to achieve that goal.

Try this method next time: "Henry, I want you to pick up all the socks and put them in your bottom drawer." Guess what? When you return everything else is still scattered all over, but you won't see any socks. Now you can continue, saying, "Henry pick up all the toys and put them in this corner." This principle is also true for statements such as "Behave," "Do well in school," "Don't get in any trouble," and so on. Kids don't know what you are talking about when you describe a goal. Even if they do understand the goal, they wonder why it is suddenly so important. If a clean room is such a big deal, why isn't it clean already? When you manage little Henry with activities, he learns where to put his socks, toys, and everything else. Eventually he learns how to keep his room clean all the time (this may not happen until shortly before little Henry leaves home). If you want your kids or anyone else to follow your management lead, the answer is management by activity. Activities are ongoing processes that are the journeys to take you wherever it is you want to go.

Loyalty Is a Journey, Not a Destination

Having loyal customers is not a goal, it is a journey—a continuous process. Customers do not sign an oath stating their intention to buy from you again and again. You must forever commit to the activities that create loyalty. This commitment is a process, an ongoing journey. When you commit to the process of creating customer loyalty, you are committing to developing and refining the activities that create loyalty.

I am not suggesting that goal-setting is not a worthwhile endeavor because it certainly is; however, goal-setting is only useful when our goals are consistent with our purpose. Goals tell us where we are going and the accomplishment of goals tells us what we have achieved. Goals inspire us and they are a means of measuring our successes. Goal setting is a worthwhile endeavor. However, goal setting is only useful when our goals are consistent with our purpose.

Too often companies place signs exhorting employees, "Build Customer Loyalty." This recognizes customer loyalty as a goal, not an activity. Companies must remember that creating loyalty isn't a destination, it is a journey.

Micromanagement

Before we begin our journey of creating customer loyalty, let me share a few thoughts about micromanagement. Micromanagement is that phenomenon where workers at every level are driven by management to accomplish tasks. Micromanagement strips the worker of creativity and self-initiative because micromanagers attempt to tell workers what to do and how to do it. Micromanagers only recognize workers for the completion of a task or series of tasks and they do not recognize workers as knowledgeable, skillful, unique resources. Micromanagers only recognize one path to accomplishment.

When you examine the activities that create loyalty, it is important to understand that these activities are interpersonal skills. No two individuals will exercise these activities in the same way. Creating loyalty is the application and an appreciation of our uniqueness. The activities that are described do not suggest micromanagement. Quite the opposite: the application of these principles should be rich with your personality, skills, and unique talents. Creating loyalty is based on recognizing your customers and business as evolving, dynamic, singular entities.

Summary

✓ Creating customer loyalty is the single most important endeavor of every business because loyal customers are the source of all profit. Loyal customers cost less to attract, are easier to deal with, and are more predictable. These benefits are the reason all profit comes from loyal customers.

✓ Customer loyalty is not an emotion or an opinion; it is an activity. Customer loyalty is the specific activity of your customers buying from you or recommending you to others on a repeat basis.

✓ The value of customer loyalty is not situational or temporary; loyal customers are always valuable. Customer loyalty is never a problem; it is always the solution.

✓ Customers who refer their family and friends to your business are your advocates and their recommendations are more valuable than any advertisement you can buy.

- ✓ Cheerleading and exhortations will not build customer loyalty. Management by activities is the only pathway to creating loyalty.
- ✓ Customer loyalty creates money. When businesses compete and customers move from one business to another and never demonstrate loyalty, none of the competing businesses win. No profit is earned until a customer returns to buy from you again and again.
- ✓ The five principles that create customer loyalty are:
  1. People do business with people
  2. Differentiation
  3. Value and assurance
  4. Effective communication
  5. Focus

Creating customer loyalty is a journey, not a destination. Getting your customers to buy from you again and again is the source of all your profit. Do you need to create more loyalty in your clientele? Take this test and see.

Loyalty Growth Lesson

1. Does every one of your customers have the ability to deliver a powerful 30-second commercial for your business?
2. Do you see your business growing every month, on a continual basis?
3. Are you financing the growth of your business solely with profits from your business?
4. Is the majority of your advertising budget and promotions directed at current customers?
5. Do you know if your customers are referring new customers to your business?
6. Do you have a program for recognizing or rewarding your customers?
7. Do you know the difference between internal and external customers?

8. Do you know why each of your customers buys from you rather than from your competitors?

9. Are the profits from your business predictable and sufficient?

10. Is your workplace free of signs such as, "Build Customer Loyalty" or "Increase Sales"?

Your answers to these questions should help you discover your strengths and weakness and alert you to what you are doing well and which areas need improvement.

Chapter 2

The Story of Customer Loyalty

Many books that claim to deal with customer loyalty are actually centered on customer satisfaction. These books promise loyal customers if the reader will only achieve a high level of customer satisfaction.

Customer satisfaction is an opinion, and the only activity associated with customer satisfaction is the completion of a survey. Customer loyalty is the activity of your customers buying from you repeatedly. It is important to note that satisfaction and loyalty are two different things.

When I appear at seminars and workshops, I first ask my audience to raise their hands if they are concerned about customer satisfaction. Most of those in the audience usually respond by raising their hands. Then I ask them to raise their hands if they have a customer loyalty program in place. Invariably there is a pause and then someone hesitantly asks, "Aren't they the same?"

I assure my audience that customer satisfaction and customer loyalty are not the same and then I ask them to participate in an exercise. For the exercise I ask them to write down their last 10 business transactions. I want them to write down where they made the purchase, not what they actually purchased. For example, if they bought a can of soup, they would write the name of the grocery store. If they bought a car, they write down the name of the dealership. I give the audience a few minutes to complete their lists. People generally write down the name of their barbershop, a car dealership, an airline, or perhaps a Realtor or a restaurant.

When they finish that part of the exercise I ask the audience to put a check mark by each vendor with which they have done business more than once. I ask them to put two check marks by vendors with which they do business on a regular basis. When they have finished, I ask them, "How pleased are you with these businesses? Did you get what you expected? Did you have to wait in line? Were the bathrooms dirty? Was the food cold? Was the food prepared the way you ordered it? Was the clerk attentive? Did your luggage go to Denver while you were traveling to Omaha? Did the bank send the right forms?"

Most often my audience will tell me that for more than half of their last 10 business transactions they really weren't totally satisfied. They felt like their satisfaction was, at best, relative. It wasn't so bad that they would never return, but they didn't feel any compunction to return. Yet these same businesses that they claimed they were not satisfied with are the businesses that have two check marks next to them. They're not satisfied but they continue to be loyal (repeat) customers! The folks who complete this exercise also learn that they do not necessarily buy again from businesses where they were very satisfied. They were satisfied but they are not loyal! The point is, customer satisfaction does not equal customer loyalty. Loyalty and satisfaction are two different things and most businesses are really interested in creating loyalty.

Your understanding of how to create customer loyalty must start by knowing you cannot create loyalty in your customers by focusing on customer satisfaction. The things you do to create customer satisfaction are not the same things you need to do to create customer loyalty.

This is not to say that customer satisfaction is not a worthy goal, but don't expect your customers to be loyal solely on the basis of their satisfaction. Keep in mind that satisfaction is relative. Customers may continue to buy from you when they are not totally satisfied, but seldom will they buy from you when they are totally dissatisfied.

While customer satisfaction is not one of the five principles that compel customers to come back, it can be a supporting asset of the principle Value and Assurance. We'll talk more about value and assurance in Chapter 5, but for now you may want to consider customer satisfaction only as a validating element of Value and Assurance. I am not suggesting that you totally ignore customer satisfaction but I am saying that there are only five principles that create customer loyalty.

Now when we reexamine the results from the "last 10 business transactions exercise" it becomes more apparent why buying habits and satisfaction levels do not match up. At best, customer satisfaction is only a supporting reason why someone becomes a loyal customer. A business could score 100 percent on customer satisfaction, but score poorly on the principles that really do create loyalty. Then, as the results from my audience show: people may be satisfied, but do not return to become loyal customers.

Loyalty Is Not Situational

Customer loyalty is beneficial to all businesses, and no business is exempt from those benefits. All businesses gain from predictability, the reduced cost to attract customers, and the ease of doing business. However, sometimes it may be difficult to see how repeat purchasing can apply to your business.

Stores that sell major appliances might not expect to see their customers return for 10 or 15 years. Is customer loyalty a realistic goal for this type of business? Residential building contractors do not anticipate building homes on a regular basis for the same buyer. Is loyalty important to this type of business? Does a surgeon expect or even want to see the same patient return again and again for additional surgeries?

Custumarius

To best understand the value of customer loyalty to your business, consider the definition of a customer. The word *customer* comes from the Latin word custumarius, which means "a person whom one has to deal." Loyal customers are not just the folks standing in front of your cash register paying you money, they are all the people you deal with on a regular or repeat basis.

You have both internal and external customers. For our discussion we'll call people standing in front of your cash register external customers—the traditional customer. They pay you or your business money for the products and services you bring to the marketplace.

Internal Customers

Internal customers are all the other folks with whom you deal. Internal customers might be your suppliers or vendors. A building contractor deals with subcontractors and is dependent on those people to complete the building project. Subcontractors are the internal customers of the building contractor. If you work for a large corporation, your internal customer might be your boss or other people that depend on the work you do. If you work in the mailroom, the people to whom you deliver mail are your internal customers. You may work in the accounting department, and so your internal customers are those who rely on your reports. By using the Latin meaning of customer, you will find that you have many more customers than what is evident at first.

You may work for a company where you seldom meet with external customers. All your dealings might only be with internal customers, but you can still benefit from applying the principles that create loyalty to the internal people. You benefit when your internal customers are predictable and they are easy to do business with. More importantly, a loyalty relationship with internal customers identifies you in the most positive manner.

Woody Allen, the film actor and director, said, "Ninety percent of life is showing up." Harrison Ford admitted in an television interview with James Lipton of *Inside the Actors Studio*, that he owes a great part of his success to just being in Hollywood when he got his big break. When the studio was casting the part of Han Solo for the movie *Star Wars*, most of Ford's contemporaries had already given up hope on an acting career and had left Hollywood. Ford feels that he got the job because he showed up to the audition. Harrison Ford may have gotten the job because he showed up, but he was also prepared.

People get jobs and promotions, and advance in their careers for showing up. Showing up may be 90 percent of life, but your chances improve when you show up well equipped. Showing up as an actor, accountant, lawyer, programmer, or anything else gets you in the arena for consideration; but showing up equipped might be why you are chosen. Showing up as someone rather than something is your opportunity for being equipped. Coco Chanel, the extraordinary fashion designer, said, "How many cares one loses when one decides not to be something, but to be someone."

A relationship of loyalty is pertinent for internal as well as external customers. The relationship of loyalty distinguishes you as someone, not a something. There are rewards for applying the principles of loyalty to everyone with whom you deal.

In the next chapter, we will be discussing the concept that "people do business with people." Ultimately, people are loyal to people. Customers may continue to trade on a repeat basis with a business, but it is the people who make up that business and who create loyalty. Internal customers are dependent on the work you do, product you provide, and the services you offer. Creating loyalty is the way for you to "show up."

Working With Internal Customers

Frank is a residential building contractor in Columbus, Ohio, who has been building homes since the 1970's. When Frank started in business it was a builder's market. Columbus was growing and there were more people looking for new homes than there were homes available. Frank's biggest challenge was finding the best subcontractor to help him build quality homes.

During the construction of Frank's first few homes he experienced every sort of problem that can plague someone new to the construction business. Some workers showed up late or didn't show up at all. Building materials were delivered at the wrong time, and then these materials sat uncovered, were damaged and had to be replaced. The drywall workers arrived before the carpenters and had to be re-scheduled. Frank's first construction site looked like a war zone. The ability to finish a building project on time with the fewest callbacks to rework or repair construction made the difference in the profitability of a project. Frank knew that finding good plumbers, electricians, masons, drywallers, and other subcontractors would be of great importance to his success. Gradually he learned which subcontractors would show up on time and do quality work.

Frank survived his problems and he continued to build homes using those subcontractors he knew he could depend on. As a building contractor, Frank was ultimately selling the cumulative work of his subcontractors to a buyer. He developed loyalty with these subcontractors and was rewarded with their *predictability* and the *ease of doing business* with them.

By the late 1970s, high interest rates were reaching historically high levels. The builder's market became a buyer's market. Frank built homes on a speculative basis. He didn't have a buyer when he began construction. Earlier this had worked to his benefit because new home prices were rising and Frank saw his building projects increase in value during construction. He had built homes, acted as his own sales agent, and had profited handsomely. Now with the shift to a buyer's market, Frank's fortune was changing. In this new market he was paying high interest rates on construction loans and buyers were getting scarce.

For the first time in his construction career Frank contacted a Realtor to help him sell his property. He could no longer just stick a sign in the yard and expect to sell the property. He was going to have to spend some money on attracting a customer. The Realtor's commission was the cost of attraction.

Today Frank's two sons have joined him in the family business. Their business is prospering beyond their fondest dreams. They depend on subcontractors, architects, land developers, Realtors, and all others with whom they deal. The loyalty Frank and his sons have created with these internal customers guarantees their continuing success.

The principles that create loyalty and the benefits from having loyal customers are the same whether they are your internal or external customers. Knowing how to deal with the customer, predictability, and the cost of attraction are just as pertinent to dealing with internal customers as they are in dealing with external customers.

Who Is the Customer?

Discovering who the customer is can be a worthwhile investigation. Sometimes even external customers are not obvious. In business-to-business commerce, the people who use a product or service may not be the same people that make the purchasing decision. Many times committees or purchasing agents are the decision-makers for large purchases such as computers or telecom services.

Julian is a senior purchasing agent for a major pharmaceutical manufacturer. He makes purchasing decisions on information technology hardware and service contracts. His decisions are based on proposals, bids, and the criteria that are established by the people that use the equipment and services he is charged with buying. Usually the vendor companies and salespeople are constantly in touch with Julian when a contract is being renewed or new purchases are being made. Between purchases or renewals these same vendors and salespeople do not do anything to create loyalty with Julian. They spend their time developing relationships with the folks that use their services or equipment. If all things are equal, Julian chooses the vendor with the lowest cost that meets the bid specifications. But all things are never really equal. They only appear equal because the salesperson or account executive has not spent time in learning what the customer values and then demonstrating the unique advantages of their solution. Most importantly, purchasing agents and committee members are also influenced by the principles that create loyalty. Effectively communicating with these decision-makers on a regular basis will create a relationship of loyalty that becomes one of the reasons why all things are not equal.

Steve and his family own and operate the Happy Times Carnival out of Kansas City, Missouri. Steve inherited the business from his father. When Steve's father ran the business the family traveled from town to town for nine months every year. While the carnival was operating in one town Steve's father would race ahead to the next town to try to find a place to set up. Occasionally, Steve's father could make arrangements to set up at the same shopping center or parking lot every year, but for the majority of their engagements every town was a new venue. Steve's father was solely concerned with having his customers come back several times during a five-day engagement. The value of customer loyalty beyond each engagement was not part of his thinking. Steve's father made a living, but never reached his potential.

Today Steve and his family provide a turnkey carnival for churches, businesses, and shopping centers. Their services include rides, games, and concessionaires. Their external customers are the patrons of the carnival: the little kid with a quarter in his hand wanting to ride on the carousel. By the time they return to a town again the next year, the little boy (their external customer) is a year older and doesn't have any interest in riding on the carousel. Steve and his family are certainly interested in providing a safe and fun environment for their external customers, but they are even more interested in their true customer, the business, church, or school that hired them. By applying the five principles that create loyalty, Steve's family business has grown and prospered beyond what Steve's father could have ever imagined.

The point here is not to define every person with whom you come into contact as a customer; however, it is important to identify internal and external customers. You can maximize the value of every business relationship by expanding your definition of "customer" to include everyone you want to deal with on a repeat basis as a "customer." It is the prerogative of every business, business owner, entrepreneur, and everyone else who is in business to enjoy the benefits of loyal internal and external customers. Each of the five principles is applicable to every business. And although every business won't use the same activities to create loyalty, every business can develop specific activities that support the five principles.

Every Business Can Benefit

The *Harvard Business Review* has a reputation for being the source of the best new ideas for people creating, leading, and transforming business. Since its founding in 1922, the *Harvard Business Review* has a proud tradition of being the world's preeminent business journal, being on the publishing cutting edge, and having authoritative thinking on the key issues facing business managers. The *Harvard Business Review* carries on that tradition today with more vigor and conviction than ever, providing its readers with engaging articles that provoke both thought and action.

However, even this august journal occasionally misses the mark. In an article titled "The Mismanagement of Customer Loyalty," published in the *Harvard Business Review* in July of 2002, authors Werner Reinartz and V. Kumar claimed:

- ✓ Much of the common wisdom about customer retention is bunk.
- ✓ The link between loyalty and profit is weaker than expected.
- ✓ The gospel of customer loyalty has been repeated so often and so loudly that it seems almost crazy to challenge it. But that is precisely what some of the loyalty movement's early believers are starting to do.

These writers confused behavior with attitude and customer management with customer loyalty. They made their evaluation based on the attitudes of customers rather than on the behavior of the customer returning to do business on a repeat basis. They further judged the profitability of repeat customers by measuring revenue rather than true costs or profits.

Customer loyalty isn't about opinions, beliefs, or attitudes. Customer loyalty is about behavior. It is the specific behavior of buying again and again from the same business while telling the world why everyone else should also buy from them. The three benefits to dealing with loyal customers are the same for every business:

- ✓ Loyal customers are predictable. Your staffing, inventory, growth, and hours of operation become easier to manage when you can predict your customers' buying habits. Customer predictability reduces operational expenses.
- ✓ Loyal customers are already doing business with you, so you don't have to attract them. The expense of attracting customers is canceled or reduced.
- ✓ Loyal customers are easier to do business with. You already know their buying habits and preferences. They know your credit terms, locations, what you sell, and a million

other things. Doing business with loyal customers takes less time.

Predictability, reduced cost of attraction, and ease of doing business are advantages to every business. It doesn't matter if you are selling McDonalds hamburgers or a McDonald-Douglas aircraft.

I hear business and sales professionals say that customers who had dealt exclusively with them for many years are now doing business with their competitors. These folks have come to the conclusion that "people just aren't loyal anymore."

Human nature is the same today as it has been throughout human history. Today people are just as loyal or disloyal as they have always been. The good news is that your behavior as a sales professional, healthcare provider, business owner, or entrepreneur is what determines their behavior as a customer. You can *create* loyalty.

I am blessed with the opportunity of working with people from all different walks of life and endeavors. Invariably after one of my presentations someone will say, "I have worked very hard to provide a quality service to my customers. I have bent over backwards to serve some of my clients and then they do business with someone else. People just aren't loyal anymore."

I gently respond, "Providing quality service is an admirable thing to do. Bending over backwards to help a customer is admirable. But quality service and bending over backwards are not one of the five principles. If you want to create loyalty you must tailor your activities around the five principles."

I recently addressed a group of businesspeople in the Southwest. After my presentation an accountant said, "People in this part of the country are different. They move here to retire. Their allegiances are back where they came from. They'll pat you on the back one day and the next day use somebody else's services. You can't create loyalty with someone like that."

I told this accountant, "The folks you're talking about are loyal. They are loyal to another accountant. People do business with people. If you consistently do the specific activities that support the five principles, they will be patting the other accountant on the back and doing business with you." The five principles can work for you just as they have worked for many others.

In an effort to bolster profits, some companies reduce their workforce, close divisions, or sell off assets. These methods are at best temporary fixes for lagging profits. They make the balance sheet look better this quarter or this year but when you lay off workers, close divisions, and sell off assets, you are also laying off, closing, and selling off productivity. These tactics usually mark the beginning of a long spiral downward. Companies that rely on the tactic of downsizing will either eventually save their way out of business or will have to turn their ship around and become more productive. Customer loyalty is the answer. Loyal customers create profit and reduce expenses.

Throughout history, captains of industry have said it was their people or workforce or employees that made a difference. They have all claimed that their people were special. Henry Ford said, "Take away the buildings and the money, but leave me with my workers and I'll have everything back in five years." Tom Watson of IBM, Alfred Sloan of General Motors, and Jack Welch of General Electric have basically said the same thing. I think they are wrong; well, at the very least I think they misspoke.

If their people were so special they would have been special someplace else before they ever arrived at Ford, General Motors, IBM, or General Electric. What made these companies great and allowed their personnel to be successful were the systems and processes used by these companies. These companies teach the activities that create success.

No company has a claim on better people. The pool of people to recruit from is the same or similar for everyone. Great companies teach their people how to improve their skills. Great companies, through their workforce activities, earn excellence and success. Wherever you are currently working, you have the ability to substantially improve your performance by learning and using the activities that create customer loyalty. It doesn't matter if you are the top dog or just starting out. The five principles that create customer loyalty are supported by activities you can use at any stage of your business maturity.

The law of life is the law of belief. People don't always get what they want, but they do always get what they truly expect. Your belief in your own success will determine your success. Some people say,

"I'll believe it when I see it." You will, in fact, "see it when you believe it." This isn't a word game or a mind trick. Those that only "believe when they see" are actually "seeing only what they believe." (We will discuss more about this phenomenon of the law of life in Chapter 7.) You will see loyal customers when you truly understand and believe in the five principles and the activities that support them. There are perhaps very few truly special people in business today. Most of us are no better or worse than those we compete against. The thing that determines our individual success is our belief in ourself and our willingness to take action on those beliefs.

Customer Relationship Management

As I write these words today, many businesses are spending enormous amounts of money on customer relationship management (CRM) projects. Customer relationship management is the tracking and collection of customer data and it provides demographic information about customers and their buying habits. Companies hope their customer relationship management project will help them create customer loyalty because they want their customers to buy from them on a repeat basis. For the most part, customer relationship projects are not working.

At the end of 2002, Lexmark, a printer company, issued a revised earnings report. The report included an "asset impairment" related to the "abandonment of a customer relationship management software project." Lexmark said it would write off $15.8 million for the failed project. Lexmark is not alone; many large businesses experience dismal results from their customer relationship management projects.

The underlying problem isn't the lack of a need to manage customer relationships. The problem is that no software or machine or any kind of equipment can take the place of personal interactive skills in developing customer loyalty. The typical actions that come about as a result of customer relationship management projects are telephone solicitations and direct-mail advertising. The material results of these efforts are no greater than telephone solicitation and advertising to non-customers. Customer relationship management programs and projects have become just another way of offering customers an additional opportunity to buy products. People aren't loyal because you are persistent in asking them to buy; loyalty is a response to the applications of interpersonal skills.

Customer relationship management projects can't produce results unless they are based on the activities that support the five principles that create loyalty. When companies put the same amount of effort into teaching, training, and equipping their employees with critical interpersonal skills that they have put into customer relationship management projects, then they will see results.

Loyal customers are the single most important asset of every company. Loyal customers are more important than land, buildings, patents, or anything else. It's the customers that bring the money. Because of the three advantages of *cost of attraction, predictability*, and *ease of doing business* only loyal customers can produce profits for your business. Land, buildings, patents, and everything else are liabilities until customers bring their money. Companies with a loyal customer base enjoy greater profit in good economic times and can depend on their loyal customers to help them survive difficult financial conditions.

It's not just about profit. The purpose of every company should be to provide value—not just for the owners but the employees and customers as well. Nearly 40 percent of all the companies on the 1990 Fortune 1000 list did not make the 2000 Fortune 1000 list. All of the companies on the 1990 Fortune 1000 list were profitable, but not all of these companies continued to provide value. Creating a loyal customer base is a demonstration of providing value.

As we discuss the five principles, you will notice that they are interrelated. For example, *effective communication* recognizes that *people do business with people*, and *value and assurance* is a *differentiator*. Each one of the principles is woven into the others.

This is the story of why some businesses enjoy tremendous success while other businesses never reach their potential. This is the story of customer loyalty and, more importantly, what you can do to develop loyal customers.

Loyalty is not an emotion, nor is it a feeling or an opinion. Customer loyalty is not dependent on customer satisfaction. Customer loyalty is an activity: The activity of your customers buying from you again and again while they encourage their family and friends to do the same.

Every business depends on repeat customers for profit. The number one question for every company doing business today should be, "How do I get my customers to keep coming back?" The answer to that question is what this book is all about. The way to keep customers coming back is simple. It's not easy, but it is simple.

Before we examine the principles that create customer loyalty in more detail, let me introduce you to the cast of characters that build customer loyalty in this book: you. The person that develops customer loyalty is the salesperson, the customer service representative, the clerk, and the delivery person. It is anyone and everyone that has any contact with the person buying, renting, leasing, or otherwise doing business with your company. When you're one-on-one with your customer, you have the opportunity and power to create customer loyalty. It is also important to note that everyone has contact with customers. An internal customer might be your boss or someone else you work with. Your customer is anyone who relies on you for a product or a service.

Summary

- ✓ Customer satisfaction is an opinion. The only activity associated with customer satisfaction is the completion of a survey. Customer loyalty is an activity; it is the activity of your customers coming back to buy from you again and again. Satisfaction and loyalty are two different things.
- ✓ There are thousands of things you can do to impact customer satisfaction. There are only five principles that you must support to create customer loyalty.
- ✓ Customer loyalty is beneficial to every business. No business is exempt from the benefits of loyal customers. The benefits of customer loyalty are: reduced cost of attraction, ease of doing business and predictability.
- ✓ The principles of creating loyalty are applicable to both internal and external customers.

Chapter 3

People Do Business With People

People don't do business with storefronts, equipment, products, or anything else: People do business with people. Loyalty is the activity of doing business with the same people again and again. This activity is the sole basis of the loyalty relationship between customer and business. Remember, loyalty isn't an opinion or an emotion, it is only an activity. However, the activity of repeat buying is a response to the specific application of interpersonal skills. This relationship is strengthened as interpersonal skills are used and adapted to various purchasing situations.

Several years ago I attended a presentation where Lee Iacocca told a story that confirms this principle. At that time, Mr. Iacocca was the CEO of the Chrysler Corporation, and he told the story about one of his executive engineers. The executive engineer was having problems meeting deadlines and was complaining to his boss, Mr. Iacocca. The executive said, "I don't have any trouble with the engineering work. It's the people that are driving me crazy." Iacocca snapped back, "People! You're just having trouble with people? Hell, that's all we have around here are people." Mr. Iacocca was saying that without people, there is no business.

Businesses look as if they are made up of buildings, machines, inventories, and supplies, but the heart and soul of every business is the people. It is people that do the work, and it is people that buy products and services. How you deal with people is the most important factor in determining your success. It doesn't matter how complex the product might be, 80 percent of your success will be determined by your people skills and only 20 percent of your success will be determined by your technical skills.

People Only Do What They Want to Do

There is only one way to get someone to do anything, and that is by making the person want to do it. You can make your children want to do something if you yell at them long enough and loud enough. You can make your children want to clean their room if you offer them a big enough reward. No matter the threat or the prize, they will not do anything unless they want to do it. No one has to do anything except take up space and die; everything else is optional.

So why do people do the things they do? Abraham Maslow, Sigmund Freud, Carl Jung, and many other great scholars of the human condition tell us that only two forces motivate people: the sex urge and the desire to be important. Some scholars claim that both of these desires are the same; ultimately, people are motivated by a need to be important. Positive expressions of importance are demonstrated by the success of our children, our financial success, the visibility of our accomplishments, our titles, and as many other things as there are people.

Because 80 percent of our success is based on our people skills, it is critical that we understand what each of our internal and external customers believe to be an expression of his or her importance. Understanding how a person wants to demonstrate his or her importance is the basis of knowing how to make someone want to do something. Listening with our ears, our eyes, and an open mind is the only way to gain this understanding. We will discuss listening a little later in this chapter and more fully in Chapter 8.

Question: *If loyalty is only buying from the same business over and over again, can a vending machine have loyal customers?*

The short answer is yes. However, even with vending machines, customers notice how well the machine is stocked, the cleanliness of the machine, and the selection. The human element is noticeably important even in the vending machine business.

Al owns a vending route in Atlanta's business district. He personally fills soda and candy machines six days a week. Al really likes his job: He has made a good living and enjoys meeting new people and old friends on his route.

Al's schedule is predictable and he knows which buildings and floors he will deliver to each day of the week. He sees many of the same people each week as he visits break rooms, kitchens, and lunchrooms around the city. It is not unusual for Al to chat with workers in these locations as he fills his vending machines. If chips or crackers have a freshness date that are close to expiration, Al leaves these products on a table for his customers. Al says that he would rather give them away than throw them away.

The office buildings that are on Al's Saturday route are usually nearly vacant. A few years ago, Al noticed that he never did as much business at the buildings he delivered to on Saturdays as the places he delivered to on weekdays. He knew the businesses had just as much traffic, but they didn't use his vending machines as much. Al changed his route and began making deliveries to his Saturday businesses on a weekday. He was visible to workers in those buildings and his sales increased to the same level as his other locations. Al now rotates his deliveries so his customers see him five out of six weeks. Even in the vending machine business people do business with people.

People doing business with people is the cornerstone principle of creating customer loyalty. All of the principles that create loyalty, which will be discussed in later chapters, are based on the interaction of people. Loyalty is a response to these interactions. People are the heart and soul of all commerce—not buildings, products, patents, or anything else.

Wendy Keller of ForthWrite Literary Agency and Speakers Bureau is my agent. I love her dearly. She has helped me develop as a writer and a public speaker. Her probing questions always help both of us understand the subjects that I research.

While I was writing this book, Wendy told me that she did most of her shopping in one department store. She said there were other stores in her area that sold the same brands at the same prices, but she preferred the one store because it had windows that looked out onto the street. She told me that the people who work there have nothing to do with her decision: It was only the windows that attracted her. There was nothing special about the store, she just preferred shopping there because she could look out the window and see the street. Wendy confessed that her behavior indicates she is loyal, but it's not about people doing business with people. She chided me, "What does that do to your principle, big shot?"

Wendy was really describing the lack of personal contact. No store in her area was offering her the opportunity to do business with people. She did not have quality contact with people, so she shopped where a store building pleased her and made her feel comfortable. In effect, her repeat buying was in default of no one offering her a reason to do business elsewhere.

A store clerk that understands the principles of loyalty would introduce herself to Wendy. She would ask Wendy questions regarding her brand and style preferences. She would point out the merits of the store's selection. She would capture Wendy's contact information, and she would send Wendy a note or postcard to thank her for visiting the store. The store clerk would notify Wendy when there is a special sale or new inventory is delivered. She would make sure Wendy's size and preferences are available.

Wendy shops where she does because no one in her area is doing anything to create loyalty. The businesses in her area do not demonstrate to Wendy that she is important. Consequently, Wendy bases her loyalty on store windows because the businesses in her area do not give her a choice to do business with people.

All things being equal, people want to do business with people they like and who like them. All things being unequal, people still would rather do business with people they like and that like them.

Businesses traditionally compete on issues such as location, price, products, and selection. The best competitive tool isn't any of these things: The best competitive tool is genuinely caring about people and making them feel important.

Customers love to find a business that recognizes them by name and gladly welcomes them when they come through the door. Customers will drive extra miles, pay more money, and buy your products if you make them feel important. Of course you better have the products and selection they want if you sincerely believe they are important.

Responsiveness Makes People Feel Important

People want responsiveness in their business transactions. When a customer does business with someone they like and who likes them back, there is an exchange. The customer feels the businessperson is sincerely paying attention to them as a person and it makes them feel important. Responsiveness is a demonstration of importance. The customer feels the businessperson is being responsive to them because they as a customer are important.

Responsiveness is an activity between people. Objects and things are directive; only people are responsive. Customers are ultimately loyal to people, not products, because of this human response.

Since the mid-1980s, most businesses have been using automated telephone systems. "Hello. You have reached Acme Industries. If you know the extension of the person with whom you wish to speak, enter that extension at any time during this message." This is a more efficient method of directing a call. One messaging system can handle thousands of calls a day. Messaging systems are directive, not responsive. A caller can direct the system, but the system is not responsive to the caller. When the customer calls and knows the extension number of the party she is trying to reach, everything is fine. When that person is not in or she wants to reach someone else and doesn't know the extension number, things are not so fine. The telephone system is directive not responsive.

People are motivated by the desire to be important. Responsiveness from interactive activities assures customers they are important.

My wife, JoyAnn, works at the Philharmonic Center for the Arts. The Phil, as it is known, is a magnificent campus including an art museum and performing arts center. Hundreds of customers and patrons call The Phil's customer service center every day to order tickets, subscribe to performance series, and make donations.

The Phil is a state-of-the-art facility but on occasion things do go wrong. Customers don't get the seating or tickets they requested or exchanges need to be made. Sometimes a customer calls and says they have called once or twice before and they still haven't received their correct order. In these situations, JoyAnn informs the callers that they should remember her name. She says, "My name is JoyAnn. I want you to remember my name. I want you to ask for me if you have a problem and need to call back." Dissatisfied customers immediately recognize that JoyAnn is the solution. Instead of being irate or irritable, they become open and friendly. JoyAnn is responsive: Customers are no longer doing business with The Phil, they are doing business with JoyAnn.

Only people can be responsive to each other, and it is this responsiveness that creates loyalty, but there are a few apparent exceptions where a product enjoys a high level of loyalty. These exceptions can always be traced back to people being responsive to people.

Morton Salt and Philadelphia Cream Cheese are examples of products that enjoy tremendous customer loyalty. Buyers for these products would not consider buying any other brands.

If we look closely, we find that both of these products enjoy an incredibly high recommendation rate from parents and family members who teach children what products to buy and use. If you ask friends and neighbors, you will find it is very common to see handwritten recipes that specify the use of Philadelphia Cream Cheese. The recommendation is so strong that no one wants to risk the success of their baked goods on any other brand. Approximately 75 percent of the salt buyers would never risk having their salt not pour when it rains. The popularity of and loyalty to these products are directly linked to personal recommendations. These products are exceptions: generally in the packaged consumer goods marketplace, loyalty is demonstrated for the seller not the product.

In 2001, General Motors announced that it was going to discontinue the Oldsmobile line of automobiles. Over the years, several other car companies have discontinued operations. Dealerships acquire new lines of automobiles to sell, and in many cases continue to maintain their loyal customer base. People might have been buying a Plymouth, but they were really doing business with the people at the dealership.

Their loyalty was not with the product; it was with the people from whom they bought the product.

Remember, people do business with people. Brand-name marketing can create brand awareness, but it cannot capture the value of people doing business with people. Let the marketing department design the product and the production department build it, but it's the job of the people that meet with customers to build loyalty.

Because people do business with people and there are typically multiple sources for a given product, it is critical that you develop customers that are loyal to you, at the specific company where you are doing business. It is the job of General Motors, Coca-Cola, Northwest Mutual, and every other manufacturer to build brand-name awareness. As a business owner, entrepreneur, or front-line employee, it is your job to build customer loyalty.

Loyalty is a customer's response to being liked and liking the people they do business with. The human condition is such that everyone is most concerned about their own welfare. If you want someone to like you, the quickest path to that end is to genuinely like them and be concerned about them.

A Company Built on Liking People

Dave Longaberger grew his family's basket-making business into a worldwide enterprise. Dave was the fifth child in a family of 12 children. Early in life, Dave had three strikes against him: his family was economically disadvantaged; he stuttered so badly people had trouble understanding him; and he had epilepsy at a time when the illness wasn't widely understood. However, he was well known in his hometown of Dresden, Ohio, and he was admired as a hard worker.

Dave genuinely liked people. He was a hard worker but he never worked so hard that he couldn't stop to inquire how someone was doing. Early in his career Dave owned a small grocery store and a restaurant. He made a habit of greeting his customers and asking about them and their families. Dave claimed that the secret to his success was how much he enjoyed talking with his customers—he truly liked people.

Dave revived his family's basket company in an old, abandoned warehouse, and he was expecting a loan to finance his new enterprise.

On his first day of production he had to tell the women that reported for work that his loan was not approved and he would not be able to pay them. But evidently, Dave's reputation for being concerned and sincerely interested in the people of his community was more important than his ability to meet a payroll. All the workers stayed and worked that day knowing they would not be paid or, if they were paid, it would not be for quite a while. They came into work the next day, and they came into work every day for five months—without pay! Dave's loan was finally approved and he made good on his promise to pay current as well as all back wages. The employees didn't work without pay for the company; they worked without pay for Dave.

Today the Longaberger Basket Company employs 7,000 craftsmen and craftswomen as well as 70,000 sales associates. The company has annual sales revenues of $1 billion and is listed as one of *Forbes* magazine's top privately held companies. The company was built on the premise of genuinely liking the workers and customers.

Longaberger Step-by-Step Loyalty

1. Demonstrate a sincere interest in your customers by being responsive to them.
2. Your customers will feel important in response to your interest.
3. Your customers will buy from you because you make them feel important.
4. Your customers are now very important to you and you are very interested in them.
5. Keep this cycle going and you will have a self-fulfilling prophecy of loyalty.

A couple of years ago, an information technology survey was conducted with several Fortune 500 companies. Each of the companies surveyed was spending hundreds of thousands and in some cases millions of dollars on information technology research, which discloses the best uses and types of telecommunication and computing equipment.

The information technology research arena is complex, scientific, and constantly evolving. Some research firms claim that there are major technology changes every 53 days and, therefore, up-to-the-minute research reports are critical. The importance of objectivity and a scientific methodology are also critical in this field. However, customer loyalty in this very sophisticated marketplace is earned the same way it is earned in much less technical marketplaces.

The survey asked chief executive officers and chief technologists, "What one thing would you change in the research services you are now receiving?" None of the respondents replied with a need for more accurate, timely, or in any way better or less expensive research reports. All of these executives spending piles of money said essentially the same thing, "I wish they knew more about my company and me." Even in this complex and highly technological field, the biggest concern for these captains of industry is to do business with someone that relates to them as people.

This desire of people wanting to be known and understood is demonstrated in all of our interactions. Businesspeople join civic, trade, and church organizations, and find they do business with the people that they meet in these groups. Many times we see famous movie stars, performers, and other well-known people who are surrounded in business with people with whom they grew up.

At the height of his career, Elvis Presley could have hired the best security company in the world to protect him, but instead he surrounded himself with bodyguards, musicians, and other people who he knew all his life. Elvis, famous movie stars, captains of industry, and everyone else want to be known and understood. Elvis didn't do business with the people he grew up with because he knew them; he chose those people because they knew him. People want to do business with people who know and understand them.

KUHL

All customers want the same thing: to do business with people who confirm their importance. The customer's importance is demonstrated by:

Know me.
Understand me.
Help me.
Lead me.

The acronym **K U H L** (pronounced "cool") tells your customers how important they are by **K**nowing, **U**nderstanding, **H**elping, and **L**eading them.

Know Me

Knowing can be as simple as knowing your customer's name or remembering your last transaction with them. If you don't know a new customer's name when they come into your business, make sure you ask and memorize it for the next time. They will repay your effort by coming back to buy from you again and again.

Customers love to walk into a restaurant, bank, clothing store, automobile dealership, or any business and be called by name. When you demonstrate that you know someone, you are demonstrating that they are important to you. The more you know about them, the more important they will feel. In later chapters we will discuss knowing your customer in more depth.

Understand Me

All customers want to be understood. They want to be understood so that you can lead, help, and serve them. Customers want to be thought of as important enough to have their wants and needs understood and taken care of.

A customer will not accept your leadership unless they believe you understand them, which is why understanding is the mutual starting point in making purchasing decisions. If you understand what the customer is trying to accomplish, you can lead them. You cannot help your customer plan their wedding, choose a computer, outfit a kitchen, buy a sports jacket, or make any other purchasing decision until you understand them and what they want.

When companies track the activities of their professional sales team, they find most often that a sale is made only after the prospect has been called on five or more times. This is a testimonial to the importance of understanding the customer. Customers are reassured that you really understand them only after you have taken the time to visit with them and learn about their issues and concerns.

Help Me

Customers want your assistance and they want you to make their lives easier. They want you to share your knowledge as you help them make buying decisions.

Customers react favorably when they see that you are providing alternatives and aids in helping them. Through your help and leadership, your customers will know you sincerely like them.

You help your customers when you offer to see your own products and services through the customer's eyes. Your explanation of products, applications, uses, benefits, and other relevant information are a demonstration of help.

Lead Me

People will welcome your leadership when they trust that you know and understand them. Customers recognize that you know your products and their applications. Everyone would like to know an expert in every product category that could guide and lead them to the best products and best buys. The position of expert is available to you if you know and understand your customer. If you don't demonstrate that you understand their wants and needs, you are just another seller trying to get the customer to part with his money.

Knowing, **U**nderstanding, **H**elping, and **L**eading (KUHL) can only be accomplished by people doing business with people. People want to be heard first and then understood. A customer's desire for you to be KUHL is satisfied by one set of ears listening to that one customer's wants, problems, challenges, and triumphs.

When you are KUHL, you are serving your customers. People are naturally skeptical of being sold, but this skepticism vanishes when your customers believe you are serving them.

In the words of Stephen R. Covey, from his 1989 book, *The 7 Habits of Highly Effective People*, "There is an intrinsic security that comes from service, from helping other people in a meaningful way. One important source is your work, when you see yourself in a contributive and creative mode, really making a difference. Another source is anonymous service—no one knows it and no one necessarily ever will. And that's not the concern; the concern is blessing the lives of other people. Influence, not recognition, becomes the motive."

When we are KUHL, we are serving other people. Specifically, we are serving our customers.

Listening is our pathway to being KUHL. Listening, as with speaking, is an interpersonal skill that needs to be practiced and developed. Most businesspeople have perfected their speaking skills—they know how to talk. Typically, these same businesspeople are deaf when it comes to listening skills. The purpose of listening is learning. Listening to the customer will reveal what the customer's frame of reference is, what is really important to them, what kind of goods and services they need, and how they want them delivered.

Unfortunately, most of us use the time a customer is speaking to develop the next thing we are going to say, so we are not really listening to the customer at all. We are more interested in saying something the customer will understand than understanding the customer through what they are talking about. Our listening skills are the most important tool we have in developing a loyalty relationship with our customers.

A few years ago my wife and I walked into an automobile dealership. We were greeted with, "Hello. Welcome to Beck Toyota. My name is George . How can I help you?" George spoke in a quiet staccato and held out his hand as he waited for us to tell him our names.

We introduced ourselves and told George we were interested in buying a Toyota Camry, a Mazda 626, or a Honda Accord. George asked, "Are you familiar with the Camry?" We said we had seen them but had never owned one. "Can I show you the features of the Camry?" he asked.

George walked us around the car on the showroom floor for the next 10 minutes. He was eager to answer our questions. He pointed out every feature on the Camry. He told us the number of coats of paint, how the inertia bumper worked, and the size of the tires. He would follow up each statement with the question, "Is this important to you?" He was the most thorough and patient car salesman we had ever met.

We spent 10 minutes inspecting the outside of the Camry before George suggested we sit inside the car. He conducted the interior inspection with the same thoroughness he had demonstrated with the exterior of the car.

George mentioned that if we were comparing three automobiles it was important that we understand the features of each. He did not mention anything about the other cars we were comparing to the Camry. He also did not ask us how soon we would be making our decision. He viewed his job as understanding our needs and providing leadership in helping us make our decision.

After our test drive, with George in the backseat offering instruction regarding the operation of the car, we returned to the dealership. George asked us for some information and we left.

When we got home an hour or so later we found George's message in our voice mail. "Hello, this is George of Beck Toyota. I am calling to tell you that your credit is approved to lease a Camry. You may reach me...."

George had mastered Know me, Understand me, Help me, and Lead me through his careful listening skills. He presented information and then listened intently so he could understand our evaluation of that information. We bought a Camry from George, but we moved from the area and didn't become loyal customers by buying another Toyota from him. Instead, we became loyal customers by referring people we know who still live in that area to George.

Many salespeople do not invest the time to thoroughly listen and understand their customers. George has mastered his listening skills and consistently sells more cars to loyal customers than others in his field. George is **KUHL**.

Know me, Understand me, Help me, and Lead me starts, continues, and ends by asking questions and then listening with all your heart and soul. People do business with people, and people want to continue to do business with people who care enough about them to understand them. The only way you can truly understand your customer is to continually ask them questions softly and then listen to them full blast. Customers are eager to answer questions that are asked with sincerity.

Our Emotions Control Our Listening

Question: *What prevents us from truly listening to our internal and external customers?*

Answer: *It is our emotions that prevent us from listening to and under standing another person.*

All human emotions can be divided into just two categories: love and fear. The emotion of love may take the form of honesty, comfort, beauty, fulfillment, and many other forms of contentment. The emotion of fear may take the form of envy, hate, gluttony, despair, hopelessness, and all other forms of discomfort.

Our fears prevent us from listening to and understanding our customers (as well as everyone else in our lives). Sometimes we are fearful that the person won't buy from us, like us, recommend us, and so on: Our fear is so great that we become obsessed with making the other person understand our position. We are human beings and we want to be important too. But our emotions tell us we can't be important if the other person doesn't do what we want them to.

Detachment and defenselessness are our only solutions. Because we become focused on the outcome of every encounter and transaction, we feel we must continually defend our position. We believe the customer must see our viewpoint. The customer must understand us. If instead we enter every encounter with a detachment from the results, we become empowered to truly listen and understand our customer. Through this knowing and understanding we begin to relate to our customers as people instead of just a potential sale.

Defenselessness

Defenselessness is your relinquishment of the need to persuade or convince others to your way of thinking. This may sound like an odd thing to do if you are trying to convince a customer to purchase your product. (Creating loyalty isn't about making a sale. Loyalty is an ongoing relationship with your customers.) In fact, defenselessness is actually a very powerful tool. Observe the people around you: You will see that people spend a substantial amount of time defending their thoughts, ideas, preferences, points of view, beliefs, and positions. (By substantial I mean 90 to 95 percent of their time is spent defending their point of view.)

Imagine how much intellectual energy we expend in being defensive. All of our mental powers are spent in attempting to answer any form of question or objection. We are so occupied with defending what we have to say that we forfeit the ability to hear and understand the people we are dealing with. Relinquishing our need to defend ourselves frees us to use our energy for listening and learning about our customers.

When we defend a position, we are telling the customer that our way is correct and that their way is wrong. In other words, we are telling them their ideas are wrong and are, therefore, not important.

People don't buy products because they do not have any objections; they buy the things they do because of a compelling reason to buy. Their purchase serves a purpose, is of value, or makes them feel good. Their objections are meaningless as long as there is a compelling reason to make the purchase. You can't convince someone to buy from you just by removing all the objections. Creating loyalty is dependent on the customer's feelings of importance. You will never demonstrate the customer's importance by proving you are right and they are wrong. Defending your position, whatever it is, is ultimately an attempt to prove yourself in the right and the customer in the wrong.

Detachment

Defenselessness and detachment are tools of empowerment in demonstrating your customer's importance. Detachment from the outcome of your interactions with customers is liberating. Detachment liberates you from following a prescribed course that you believe will culminate in a sale. If you are attached to the outcome, you are attached to the process. This attachment does not allow you to explore, listen, and understand the customer.

Being detached from the outcome does not mean you have lost interest in your goal of doing business or creating loyalty because your goals and intentions remain the same. However, there are infinite possibilities between point A and point B. Your detachment frees you to see all possibilities and you are less likely to force solutions on problems.

Your detachment is a signal to your customers that your interest is in them and not just completing a transaction or closing a deal. When your customers see that you have a sincere interest in them, they are more open and revealing. This openness leads to your knowing and understanding them. As long as you are attached to the outcome of your endeavors you can never be open to all the possibilities that are available to you.

Defenselessness and detachment are merely mind-sets. We can develop these mind-sets through mental reminders. Before every meeting or encounter with your customers, relinquish your need to defend your point of view and remain open to all opinions and thoughts. Rather than focusing on a rigid agenda, you should participate in everything with a detached involvement. Your customers will feel at ease, recognize your appreciation of their importance, and reward you with their loyalty.

Your greatest tool in knowing, understanding, helping, and leading is listening. By asking your customers questions and then listening to their responses, you will learn about them and you will understand them. Asking questions and listening because you sincerely want to know the answer is at the heart of customer loyalty. Defenselessness and detachment are tools to empower your listening skills.

Harvey MacKay is a great storyteller and one of the best coaches in American business. Harvey tells the story of the dog, Ole Poon. Ole Poon sits by your side nearly asleep. When you pick up the newspaper or go to the refrigerator for a beer, Ole Poon never moves. As soon as you begin to consider taking Ole Poon out for a walk he miraculously knows your intentions and is standing by the door wagging his tail furiously. How did he know? MacKay points out that Ole Poon's only job is to watch you. He knows your moves better than you know yourself. You have all kinds of things to think about and consider, but Ole Poon only has you. While you are watching Ole Poon only 1 percent of the time, he watches you 99 percent the time. That's how he makes his living.

Ole Poon doesn't have much speaking ability, but he sure can watch and listen. Ole Poon is KUHL.

Show Me You Know Me

People respond to and naturally like people that like them. People don't have to be alike to like each other; they only have to detect that they are liked. In order to like someone, you must first know them.

In some cases we don't like a person's actions in certain situations, but we like the person on the whole. The likable characters that did despicable things on Jerry Seinfeld's long-running situation comedy are examples.

"Knowing" someone is more important than the specifics of the relationship. In business, every customer subconsciously gives the command, "Show me you know me. If you 'show me you know me,' then I'll know you like me." The unspoken philosophy is *you wouldn't take the time to know me if you didn't like me.*

At first blush, the notion of learning to like someone may seem contrived or artificial to you. Do we like someone just because we know and understand them? You may be thinking, "I do not care about truly liking my customers, I just want to do business with them. Liking the customer is just an act. I just want their money. I have plenty of friends. Do I need to like this guy just because he is a customer?"

Nothing in this world is inherently interesting. For example, do you play an instrument? Do you remember when you first began music lessons? There was nothing interesting about playing that instrument: your hands were uncomfortable and it sounded awful. You'd rather have been doing something else but someone made you practice. After a little while, practicing became more comfortable and there was a trace of a tune starting to emerge. As you toiled away week after week, month after month, you began to enjoy playing that instrument. As you became more accomplished, playing the instrument began to become interesting. It became fun and challenging. Today, even though you haven't touched that instrument in years, you look back with fond memories. You think, "Playing music was fascinating."

Maybe you didn't play an instrument, and even if you did, this may not be a totally accurate reflection of your experience; however, the point is little or nothing in this world is interesting until you get involved. Growing champion roses, collecting stamps, watching NFL games, motor boating, gourmet cooking, and a million other things are not interesting until we invest some time to learn about them.

Most of us won't jump up and down with excitement at the thought of learning to like someone. But much like playing the piano, if we invest a little time, we will find our interest increasing with our accomplishment. The reason we don't like someone is typically because we don't know them. Liking the people we do business with isn't artificial; it is the most natural thing in the world if we learn about them.

Joey is an inside sales executive for a major research corporation. Joey conducts all of his business by telephone and rarely meets with his customers in person. Joey primarily calls on "C" level executives. His clients are usually chief executive officers, chief financial officers, or chief information officers. These high-level executives are usually very busy and can be difficult to reach. Most of these people have a gatekeeper to run interception on salespeople, such as Joey, who attempt to call on them.

One of Joey's prospects was an executive at the prestigious Mayo Clinic in Rochester, Minnesota. Joey had tried to call this executive several times but never got through to speak to him. He left messages but his calls were never returned. Joey had called on this executive so many times that he was on a first-name basis with the gatekeeper.

One day while making yet another attempt, Joey learned that the gatekeeper would not be in to work for a few days. He asked her if she would be out on business or pleasure. She told him she was taking a few days off to plant a garden. As they chatted for a few minutes, Joey learned how much the gatekeeper enjoyed vegetable gardening. My friend told her about the Heirloom Tomato Company, which distributes tomato seeds that produce tomatoes that taste like they came out of your grandfather's garden.

The gatekeeper had not heard about Heirloom, but she was very interested. Joey told her that he had half a package of seeds left over from his garden and would send the package to her. After she received the seeds, Joey never had any trouble reaching the executive or having him return his calls. Joey demonstrated he knew the gatekeeper and followed up on what he said he would do. The gatekeeper felt recognized as a person of importance and demonstrated her authority. A dollar's worth of seeds became worth thousands of dollars in business.

Harlow Edwards left the military service at the end of World War II. He went to work for a life insurance company that also offered health indemnification policies. The indemnification policies paid $10 a day if the insured was hospitalized. Back in the late 1940s, the cost for this coverage was only a few dollars a month.

Harlow called on veterans returning home after the war. He established a goal of having 750 clients. In his first couple of years in business he wasn't truly interested in how much money he made: He was more interested in achieving his goal of 750 clients.

Harlow made sales calls and explained the benefits of life insurance. More often than not his prospect didn't buy any life insurance at all. But just before Harlow left his prospect he would stop at the door and say, "You'd buy a little bit just to be friendly, wouldn't you?" Harlow would then write up orders for the indemnification policy on the prospect and his family. During his first three years in the insurance business, Harlow sold 750 policies. The polices were written for newborn babies, housewives, husbands, and anybody else who may have been in the room. At the end of three years, Harlow declared he would never prospect again. He had identified his entire universe of clients.

Over the next 40 years Harlow socialized with every one of his policyholders at least once a year. In the early years Harlow and his wife invited policyholders to their home for potluck suppers and card games. As business improved, Harlow had a swimming pool built in his backyard where he continued to entertain his policyholders. Harlow and his wife took clients to dinners, movies, concerts, and the theater. Never prospecting but always maintaining social mobility with his universe of policyholders.

As his clients matured and prospered, Harlow was their insurance agent. Babies grew up and became professionals, teachers, business owners, and captains of industry. Harlow had known them since birth and was the person they turned to for help with their insurance.

Harlow had sold 750 policies to 250 families. He socialized with each of these families and knew dates of birth, graduation dates, anniversaries, and everyone's name. Harlow knew his customers and he made them feel important. He liked them and they knew and liked him in return. His customers knew him, but more importantly, they understood that Harlow knew them. Harlow made a fortune in the insurance business. Harlow was KUHL.

Summary

✓ People only do what they truly want to do. There is only one way to get anybody to do anything and that is by making *them* want to do it.

✓ The great scholars of the human condition tell us that people are motivated by a need to be important. This need to be important is expressed by the success of our children, visible wealth, accomplishments, and by how people respond to us.

✓ Our people skills determine 80 percent of our success, and our technical skills determine only 20 percent.

✓ People doing business with people is the cornerstone principle of creating loyalty. People are the heart and soul of all commerce—not buildings, products, or anything else.

✓ Businesses traditionally compete on location, price, products, and selection, but the best competitive tool isn't any of these. The best competitive tool is genuinely caring about people and demonstrating their importance. Responsiveness is a demonstration of importance.

✓ All customers want the same things. They want you to Know them, Understand them, Help them, and Lead them. The acronym KUHL (pronounced "cool") tells your customers how important they are.

✓ Your greatest tool in knowing, understanding, helping, and leading is listening. By asking your customers questions and then listening to their answers, you will learn about and understand them. Asking questions and listening because you sincerely want to know the answer is at the heart of customer loyalty. Defenselessness and detachment are tools to empower your listening skills.

How's your loyalty level? The following test will help you assess how well you know your customers. In Chapter 4 we will discuss how to use "differentiation" to make your business irresistible to your customers, but first take the Show Me You Know Me—Loyalty Test.

You should come back and take this test again after you read each of the chapters that describe a principle. As you progress in your quest for loyalty, you will be astounded by your increased customer knowledge.

Show Me You Know Me—Loyalty Test

1. Do you know how many internal customers you have?
2. How well do you know these internal customers? What do you really know about them besides the work they do?
3. Do you know how many external customers you have?
4. How well do you know these external customers? Can you describe these customers in terms other than through business transactions?
5. Are your internal and external customers equipped to describe you to other potential customers in terms beyond just the products or services you sell?
6. Do you genuinely like your customers?
7. What do you like about them?
8. As a customer, what do you like or admire about the people that provide you with goods or services?
9. Who is your perfect customer and why?
10. Do you make your customers feel important?

This is not a pop quiz where you get a passing score and you are finished. Your knowledge and understanding of your customers is the most important aspect of your business day. Your success in business and in life will be determined by knowing what people want so you can help them get it. If you can show enough people how to get what they want you will have everything you will ever want.

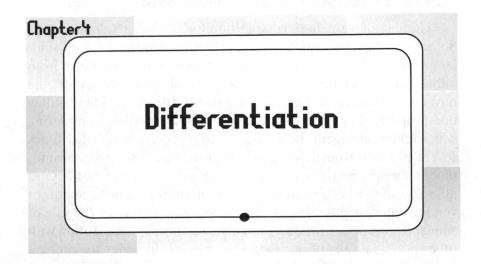

Chapter 4

Differentiation

In Chapter 2, I described an exercise I ask my audience to participate in at the workshops and seminars I conduct. The audience discovers that customer satisfaction has little to do with their buying habits. The exercise demonstrates that many times customers are loyal even when they aren't satisfied. So why do people shop where they do?

People buy what they buy where they buy it because of the value of the product or service; don't confuse value and price. Price is only one part of value. The differences in location, color, selection, service, style, and a million other things are all differentiators in products and services. These differences provide superior value and cause someone to trade with the people they do.

Differentiators make one business, product, or seller distinguishable from another. Through differentiation you are demonstrating why your customers should do business with you instead of your competitor. If there is no difference between you and the competition, your customers have no reason to choose you over the other guy.

There Is Competition for Every Sale

There is an element of competition for every purchase and sale. Sometimes the competition is between two or more sellers for a similar product. A buyer is considering the purchase of a computer from either a major retailer or a local computer shop. In real estate, the buyer is considering the purchase of a piece of property. There is only one property that interests the buyer, but she may be considering which real estate agent she would like to represent her. Other times several products from different sellers are being considered. An automobile shopper might be considering a Ford, Chevrolet, or Chrysler all from different dealerships. In some situations it's not a matter of vendors, specific products, or salespeople competing for the sale of similar or competing product, but, instead, there is competition with other potential uses of our money or capital. In order to win, you have to not only illuminate what makes your solution or product most appealing, but also make the competing product or service adverse, not as attractive, or risky. This process of competition and the buyer's final decision is always based on differentiators.

Differentiators in Commerce

When there is no appreciable difference in a product or service it becomes a commodity. Commodities are ultimately sold based solely on price. Differentiators are the unique features or differences in your product or service that make it stand out, make it special, make it anything but a commodity. In your individual situation you may not be able to differentiate your product, but you can differentiate your services and how you deal with your customer. Payment terms, delivery, and availability are the traditional differentiators for commodities; however, these differences are temporary and don't necessarily create lasting loyalty.

Gasoline is usually thought of as a commodity. There may be compelling differentiators in terms of where you specifically buy gasoline but the product itself is viewed as a commodity. You might be loyal to an individual gasoline station because of its location, hours of operation, or your relationship with the station owner, but few people are fiercely loyal to a brand of gasoline. However, a notable exception is Shell Oil.

In the 1960s, Shell Oil produced stunning advertisements featuring two identical automobiles driving in the desert. Each car had a special beaker attached to the hood. The beaker on one car was filled with Shell Oil gasoline with platformate. The beaker on the second car was filled with gasoline without platformate. The two identical cars with the same amount of gasoline took off together and traveled at the same speed.

The two cars drove through the desert for a few miles. The car fueled with the gasoline without platformate spit, sputtered, and rolled to a stop while the car with Shell Oil gasoline with platformate continued on for what seemed like a substantial distance. Finally, the Shell Oil car drove through a banner and came to rest. The announcer's voice proclaimed the benefits of Shell Oil with platformate and encouraged the audience to take advantage of this difference.

There are two reasons why this was such a stunning advertisement. The first reason has to do with the composition of gasoline. A chemist friend tells me that all gasoline of that era contained platformate. Shell Oil's scientists had to go to great lengths and expense to remove the platformate from a batch of gasoline so they could fuel the losing car in the commercial.

Secondly, and most importantly, these advertisements clearly differentiated Shell Oil from all other brands of gasoline. Even today, many years since the advertisement last appeared, many believe Shell's products to be superior. Shell's gasoline is considered a premium product. There is a difference. If people perceive a difference then there is one.

Some people may feel that Shell Oil did something dishonest or misleading by running the platformate ads, but nothing could be further from the truth. Shell Oil didn't say it was the only company that sold gasoline with platformate; in fact, the commercial didn't talk about other brands of gasoline. Shell Oil differentiated by very carefully describing its product. It differentiated by talking about the virtue of its own product.

A company that sells bottled water can differentiate by describing where its water comes from and how it is filtered. The company doesn't need to compare its product to others in the marketplace because its description of the product is a differentiator if no other competing advertisers are describing their product in the same way. The difference is that you know how one company processes its water, but you may not know how its competition processes theirs.

The brewery giant Anheuser-Busch produces Budweiser beer. Budweiser proclaims their product to be the "King of Beers." Was there a vote? Was there ascension to the throne by birthright? Budweiser tells us that its beer is beechwood aged. I don't know if all beer is beechwood aged, or even if beechwood aging is a good thing, but I do know that Budweiser is beechwood aged. Budweiser uses beechwood aging as a differentiator. Telling your customers what you do or how you do it is a differentiator unless everyone else is making the same claim.

Quality Is a Commodity

A generation ago, quality was a huge issue in the marketplace: it was a major differentiator. Manufacturers and sellers of automobiles, hardware, clothes, and appliances focused their marketing on quality. People bought quality, and they were willing to pay a premium price for it.

Modern manufacturing techniques and the global distribution of products and information has changed the value of quality. Today people take quality for granted—it is expected. Whether an automobile costs $15,000 or $50,000, it routinely operates for 200,000 miles without major repair. Appliances and clothing are replaced because of color or style before they ever wear out. Many products are replaced because of obsolescence rather than failure. While everything is better, it is also increasingly the same.

Many products are the same today as they were 50 or more years ago. Candles aren't much different today then they were 100 years ago. Manufacturing techniques may have changed, but it would be difficult to tell the difference between a brand new candle and one that was made 100 years ago.

The Massachusetts-based Yankee Candle Company has more than 30 years' experience in the candle-making business. The company advertises its 8-inch taper with a seven-hour burn time while its three-wick parlor candle will burn for 30 to 35 hours. A candle shopper can compare burn rates and style and make a buying decision. In effect, this comparison reduces quality to the status of a commodity. One 8-inch taper that burns for seven hours can't be much different from another 8-inch taper that burns for the same amount of time.

Another example of the commoditization of quality is the paper industry. Manufacturing techniques have changed drastically over the 120-year history of this industry; however, the finished product remains an 8 1/2 x 11–inch sheet. At one time, companies such as Fox River, Hammermill, and Southworth attracted their customers with their claims of quality. These companies still tout their quality, but buyers make their purchases based on price because quality is assumed. Quality in the paper industry is a commodity. Shoppers at Office Depot, or the local office-supply store narrow their searches by weight, brightness, and size. Once shoppers find 8 1/2 x 11-inch paper of the desired weight and brightness it is simply a matter of which ream costs less. Quality is a commodity. Today, quality is the minimum requirement to enter a marketplace.

One of the greatest automobiles ever built is the Acura Legend. The Legend was manufactured from 1986 to 1995. The customer satisfaction level for the Acura Legend is as high as any automobile ever tested. Owners have reported fewer problems, received better service, and continue to enjoy more comfort and efficiency than they ever expected. Owners believed the fit and finish to be world-class. The resale value for Legends remains exceptionally high. Owners loved their Legends, but unfortunately, they did not go back for a second Legend. Less than half of Legend buyers bought a second Legend. When they replaced their Legends, more often than not it was with a different brand. This illustrates that tremendous customer satisfaction does not equal customer loyalty. Remember, customer satisfaction is an opinion while customer loyalty is an activity.

Even though Legend owners were thrilled with their cars, they felt that the Lexus, Avalon, and Infiniti were comparable automobiles. The Legend owners did not see a differentiator. They asked, "What's the difference? They are all good."

Toyota, on the other hand, enjoys the highest repeat business in the automobile industry. What is so different about Toyota? Owners will tell you, "Toyotas are the most reliable cars ever built." These cars may or may not be the most reliable, but Toyota reminds their customers through regular mailings and advertising that the distinguishing characteristic of each and every Toyota is reliability. There may be other cars that are faster, sportier, bigger, and more deluxe; however, when it comes to reliability, you have to buy a Toyota.

Toyota owners are so convinced of the difference that they won't risk purchasing any other brand. While less than one half of Acura Legend owners bought another Legend, about 70 percent of all Toyota owners have returned to their dealers for another Toyota. Reliability is the differentiator.

Toyota knows that just being different is meaningless. Differentiation only works when you differentiate with value that has meaning to your customers.

Being the Best versus Being the Only One

Being the best at what you do may mean very little: It is more important to be considered the only one who does what you do.

Years ago, I had a friend that owned a small FM radio station. This was long before FM radio was the most used broadcasting system. At that time, most radio listeners tuned in to their favorite station on an AM radio. My friend's station had the smallest audience in the city where he broadcast. One day I asked him how he was able to attract advertisers with his small audience. He said, "It's simple. I don't have a big audience, but if an advertiser wants to reach my audience he has to advertise through my station. My audience isn't listening to the biggest station. They listen to my station." My friend knew back then that being the best wasn't as important as being the only one that does what you do. In this sea of sameness where even quality is not a differentiatory, how can each of us stand out from our competitors?

This Lawyer Differentiated by Being the Fastest

I met Dave Grissom several years ago. Dave is from Louisville, Kentucky. He came from a middle-class family and his father was a paint salesman. Dave's father died at a fairly young age as a result of complications from exposure to paint fumes.

Dave Grissom was not an inspired student. He graduated from the University of Louisville in the middle of his class and he was accepted at that university's law school and completed his law degree without distinction. At the time of his graduation there were a few very exclusive law firms in Louisville that hired only graduating lawyers from Ivy League schools. One of these highbrow firms decided to hire Dave to appease the University of Louisville's efforts to place one of their graduates in the local firm.

The firm hired Dave, but they did not really support him. He was given a minimal salary, but not an office. Instead he was told to work out of the firm's law library.

Young lawyers are dependent on their firm for clients. The only work Dave was given was work from clients no one else wanted: simple wills and uncomplicated divorces. He didn't earn much money and the work was not very challenging.

Dave decided that if he was going to be noticed, he had to do something noticeable. He decided he would become the fastest lawyer in Louisville. Dave would meet with a client couple to discuss their wills. They might spend half an hour to an hour with Dave and then they would leave. When they arrived home a little later, they were surprised to receive a phone call from Dave so soon. "I have the wills prepared for your signatures. When can you return to our office?" It didn't take long for Dave's reputation as the fastest lawyer in Louisville to become known. He wasn't the cheapest or the smartest, or the best or the best known, but he was the fastest. When people who knew several lawyers wanted law work done ASAP, they went to Dave.

Dave stayed with that law firm for only a short time. He wanted his own office and his reputation was helping him build a clientele. He joined two other young attorneys and opened a firm where the three lawyers shared the rent and one secretary.

The reception area, which the young attorneys referred to as the "bullpen," was horseshoe-shaped with the secretary in the middle and the three lawyers' offices surrounding her. One day the secretary entered Dave's office and announced, "There is a Mr. Brown here who would like to see you." Dave said, "Let Mr. Brown cool his heels in the bullpen for a few minutes and then show him in."

A few minutes later Mr. Brown held his hand out to Dave and said, "Hi. I'm John Y. Brown. I am the president of Kentucky Fried

Chicken and I need your help in moving our headquarters from Nashville to Louisville. I don't care about the price, but I need it done in three months. I understand you're the only lawyer in Louisville that can get it done. Can you help me?" Dave told me he was gripping the arm of his chair so tightly his knuckles were white and he couldn't let go to shake Mr. Brown's hand.

Dave and John Y. Brown continued their business relationship for many years. And Dave had his reputation for being the fastest lawyer in town to thank for that.

Dave Grissom has had a tremendous career. He and his law partners grew the Louisville-based Extendacare into Humana, the giant healthcare company. Dave went on to become chairman of a national bank and a true captain of industry. Even at the pinnacle of his career, Dave admits, "I started out by being different. When other lawyers took days or weeks, I took hours." He established a differentiator to keep his clients coming back.

Everyone can't be the fastest. Everyone can't be smartest, funniest, most experienced, or the most of anything else. Every company doesn't have the best price or the most selection or a permanent corner on innovation. However, everyone, including you and me, can develop signature traits that differentiate us. It can be as simple as developing a reputation for always returning phone calls within the day or the hour.

Lou Holtz, the national champion football coach, is known for starting every conversation with a sincere, "How can I help you?" There are as many ways to differentiate as there are people.

The purpose of this differentiation discussion is to ultimately increase loyalty in your clientele. Customer loyalty is the activity of either repeat buying or customers recommending your product or service. Even small differentiators identify you and give customers something to tell others about you.

Uniqueness

The key to differentiation is uniqueness. Telling the world that you have fast and friendly service will not differentiate you because the world is full of businesses proclaiming to have fast and friendly service.

Early in Ray Charles's legendary singing career, he was known as Little Nat. Ray sounded identical to his musical hero, Nat King Cole. Even back then when he was just starting out Ray was a terrific singer, but there was only room in the world for one Nat King Cole. Ray could play clubs and make a little money, but if he was ever going to really make a name for himself he had to become Ray Charles. When Ray discovered his own voice, his career took off like a rocket. Ray learned that the best way to differentiate was to be himself and work at being the best he could be.

A friend of mine is the president of his medical group, which produces substantial revenue. He does the group's banking at a small local bank. The bank has changed ownership several times over the years and he could get better interest rates and more services at a larger bank, but he has remained loyal. He told me, "They know my name at the bank. I know them. They care about me and my business." He suspects a larger bank would care about his money and not about him. Just caring about somebody can differentiate you from your competition.

We live in a world where every doctor is board certified, every mechanic is factory trained, all parts and service are guaranteed, all electronic consumer goods retailers will match any competitor's advertised price, everyone claims to have a friendly staff, and every grocery store has only the freshest produce and most complete selection. I am not complaining. In many ways the world is a better place than it has ever been. However, the price we pay for these universal improvements is sameness. Every city and village across the country has the same stores and restaurants. They may all be good but they are the same in Chicago as they are in Denver.

You May Be Paying Too Much

If you grew up before the 1980s, you probably remember the expression "You always get what you pay for." Typically, your mom or dad used this expression to teach you that quality has a price. A cheap watch could only be cheap. If you focused all your attention on price, you would only get junk. "You always get what you pay for" was an admonishment to pay a little extra and buy quality. The expression meant that saving a few bucks would cost more in the long run. The notion of getting what you paid for was linked to doing business with people you know and trust.

We don't hear that expression as much today. News reports, magazine articles, and even entire magazines such as *Consumer Report* are saying, "You may be paying too much." You may be paying too much for car insurance. You may be paying too much for vitamins. You may be paying too much for just about everything.

Who Are You Doing Business With?

There has been a philosophical switch. We went from having to worry about paying too little to having to worry about paying too much. To a large extent, this change is a reflection of the marketplace. Quality is better today than ever; however, we are more distanced from the people we do business with. The nationalization of businesses removes us from knowing who we are doing business with. Who are we doing business with when we shop at Home Depot or Wal-Mart? Even the funeral home business, which was once almost exclusively locally owned, has been merged by a few key players. These large businesses do little to court our loyalty. They focus on point-of-sale customer satisfaction and differentiate only by price. We are less familiar with the people we do business with. Sellers at all levels are more interested in being competitive than they are in being consultative.

Retailers that sell tires, electronics, automobiles, furniture, and appliances go through great effort to guarantee they have the lowest price but do little to help the buyer make the best choice in what to purchase. They don't want you to pay too much, but could care less about what you purchase. Stockbrokers nearly insist on discounting their fees to match the online brokers, but are offering less and less advice.

These sellers believe this is the only way to compete. They believe the customer will take their free consultative advice and then buy the product or service from the cheapest seller. They believe their best hope for competing is to lower their price and work off greater volume. And so the street vernacular becomes, "You may be paying too much."

If we want to succeed as business owners, entrepreneurs, and professionals in developing loyal customers for our enterprises, we need to offer our customers a difference. We need to develop differentiators so they'll have a reason to be loyal. The only difference we truly bring to the marketplace is ourselves.

Customers Are Buying You

The delivery of a professional service is absolutely nothing more than the delivery of you or me. The only thing Realtors, financial service professionals, accountants, lawyers, and everybody else who delivers a service are truly delivering are themselves. When a business hires me to come in and help their company, the only thing they get is me. When the famous trial attorney Johnny Cochran is hired to represent a client, the only thing they get is Johnny. When your customer hires you as an accountant, Realtor, or insurance agent, all they get is you. You may not be the product or the results, but you are the differentiator.

The Internet makes everything available to everyone. An entire town was sold on the auction site eBay. The marketplace is loaded with choices.

Question: *What's the difference between buying from the local purveyor or from someone across the country? (Your purchase will be delivered to your door.)*

Answer: *You and I are the difference.*

As a child, do you remember hearing that every snowflake is different? Snowflakes aren't very complicated. If every snowflake is different, imagine how different each of us are. A snowflake may only live till it hits the ground—we don't even begin to develop our differences until we hit the ground.

The human condition is such that each of us is unique. The subtle and not so subtle differences in each of our skills, personalities, and experiences make each one of us unique beings. No one else is just like me and no one else is just like you. Using these differences constructively in our interactions with internal and external customers is the basis for creating loyalty through differentiation.

There are only 12 different notes in the chromatic scale; however, the application of these notes has produced an endless variety of songs for all of us to enjoy. My junior high school English teacher pointed out that there are only seven basic story plots, yet the variation on these few basic plots have entertained the world since the beginning of mankind. Inside each of us is a treasure chest of differences that are available in our expression of commerce in general and dealing with our customers in specific.

Subtle differences aside, consider everyone involved in commerce to be either a worker or a manager. In the language of the law profession, lawyers are either grinders or finders. Grinders are those lawyers who do the actual legal work whether it is writing documents or appearing in court. Finders are those lawyers who bring new clients into the firm. In this simple model of commerce, I am suggesting people either manage workers (their internal customers) or they meet with external customers.

A manager's job description is much like that of an athletic coach. The coach's job consists of:

1.   Teaching the basics every day.
2.   Clearing the path of obstacles.
3.   Offering encouragement.

Managers are charged with these same tasks. The greatest athletes, musicians, magicians, artists, and artisans practice every day. Practice reinforces the basics for great basketball players such as Shaquille O'Neal and great musicians such as cellist Yo-Yo Ma. Great managers teach the basics every day. Nobody who wants to excel is exempt from reviewing the basics every day.

Coaches clear the path of obstacles for their players by offering strategy and scouting reports on the competition. Managers clear the path of obstacles by being a liaison to every department in the organization. Coaches offer encouragement either through criticism or praise—good managers do the same.

The point is that while the fundamentals of being a manager or a coach are very limited, the ways these fundamentals can be expressed are infinite. Is there a difference in the way Pat Riley and Phil Jackson coach? You bet! They both have the same job, but their individual styles and personalities are dramatically different. Bill Gates and "Chainsaw Al" Dunlap have both managed their companies to

the highest levels of business success but these executives are as different as day and night.

A manager's job is to serve internal customers. A worker's job is to serve external customers. In this simplistic model, a worker's job is to:

1. Know and understand customers.
2. Partner with customers to help them receive the best product or service.
3. Recognize and demonstrate the customer's importance.

There are as many different ways to accomplish these tasks as there are people. Imagine using your individual style and unique skills in accomplishing these tasks. Consider your specific customers, how you interact with them to know and understand them, and partner with them as you demonstrate their importance and apply your uniqueness.

People make choices in the people they do business with because they detect a difference. They come back to buy again and again because of differentiators. You are this difference when you apply your unique skills, experiences, style, concern, personality, and methods in your interactions with customers. Commerce is filled with sameness and commodities. You are one of a kind. You are the only one of you available anywhere. You are the differentiator.

Pareto's Law

Do you know about the 80/20 rule? The 80/20 rule says, "Eighty percent of all goods and services sold are sold by 20 percent of the people who sell those goods and services." Italian economist Vilfredo Pareto discovered the 80/20 rule in 1897. Sometimes the 80/20 rule is called the Pareto Principle or Pareto's Law. Whatever you choose to call it, the 80/20 rule is pretty much true of just about everything. Eighty percent of all the goods are produced by 20 percent of the manufacturers. Eighty percent of the laws are proposed by 20 percent of the lawmakers. Eighty percent of the world's resources are used by 20 percent of the world's population. Twenty percent of the criminals commit 80 percent of the crimes. I'm sure you get the idea.

Some years ago Tom Simon was the CEO of Capital Holding Company. Capital Holding is now owned by the financial services

giant Aegon. At that time, Capital Holding Company owned several insurance companies. Tom told me that his company conducted a survey to explore the 80/20 rule, believing it could have a major impact on its sales efforts. The company knew that 20 percent of its agents accounted for 80 percent of its sales. The company wanted to figure out why such a small percentage of its sales force accounted for such a large percentage of the company's annual sales. The first discovery was that 80 percent of the 80 percent of insurance that was sold was sold by 20 percent of the 20 percent that was selling insurance. The 80/20 rule even applied to the 80/20 rule. Do the math. The company's research showed that 64 percent of all the insurance being sold was being sold by 4 percent of the insurance salespeople. What could the 4 percent be doing that was so different from the rest of the salespeople?

The insurance company spent a great deal of money eliminating criteria that was not responsible for the success of the 4 percent. The elite 4 percent were not smarter, nor were they better educated. They were not younger or older, and they didn't come from better families or come from bad families. In fact, the survey uncovered nothing. Ultimately, Capital Holding sent a questionnaire to the very productive 4 percent. The questionnaire asked, "What are you doing that allows you to sell so much insurance?"

The first thing the survey revealed was that each of the salespeople that were in the 4-percent group could name at least 100 specific things they labeled as a sales technique. For example, one salesman said he only used a Mont Blanc pen to sign contracts. He said he used "an expensive pen because it makes every deal look like a big deal." Big deal! Another salesperson said he always used a cheap Bic pen because it made him look like the low-overhead price leader.

One salesman said that he always had business cards with him and another said he never carried business cards. The man who never carried business cards said, "If I give someone a business card, they say they will call me, but they never do. I tell them, 'I don't have a card but I'll call you.'" And he always does call them.

The individual techniques that the salespeople reported weren't what were most important. It was the number of techniques, not the

specific techniques that made the difference. By having specific techniques, the salespeople were demonstrating that they had thought about each aspect of dealing with their customers. They were organized and routinely did things they felt their customers would respond to or appreciate. Each of the specific techniques was a differentiator. Each technique gave their customers another way to identify and describe to others with whom they were doing business.

This is not to say that the specifics of the differentiator are totally unimportant. The differentiator needs to be appropriate to the service or product you offer. It won't help you to wear a funny hat or be known as the biggest fan of the local football team. Your differentiator needs to demonstrate how you are different, but must also be a specific benefit to your customers.

Differentiators Must Have Value

A chain of Mexican restaurants in my neighborhood advertise by proclaiming it is the Mexican restaurants in the ugly green buildings. It has differentiated themselves from all other Mexican and other kinds of restaurants by being in ugly green buildings. Unfortunately, having ugly green buildings is of no value to their clientele. The buildings might be easy to spot as you're driving by, but being easy to spot is pretty far down the list of reasons you pick a place to have dinner. After you know where a restaurant is located, the reminder that you ate in an ugly green building will do little to prompt your return.

Their advertising dollars would be better spent if they described the quality of food or selection or cleanliness. The advertisement should remind customers of the good dining experience. Your differentiator needs to distinguish you from your competitors but must also be a benefit your customer.

Segmenting the market to serve a specific group can be an effective differentiator. Established in 1983, Chico's began in a small store on Sanibel Island, Florida, with Marvin and Helene Gralnick, who sold Mexican folk art and cotton sweaters. By 2003, the Gralnick's grew their enterprise to 360 stores nationwide. Chico's prides itself on exclusive private label designs and amazing personal service.

Chico's is a unique retail environment. When a customer walks into a Chico's, she can depend on a member of the sales staff to coordinate, accessorize, and help her build a wardrobe to suit her needs. Chico's fashions are designed and developed by their own product development team, which allows them to provide their customers with new styles each week.

Chico's has clearly defined its customer profile. They cater to an upscale audience of women between the ages of 35 and 55. They have further differentiated themselves by offering clothing in only four sizes rather than the traditional eight sizes of most women's clothing stores.

Chico's has differentiated itself by how their sales staff interacts with the customers and the products they offer. The 2002 holiday season sales figures for most retailers showed very modest increases or declines in sales in the 4-percent to 15-percent range. During this same period, Chico's enjoyed a 44-percent increase in its sales. Its differentiators were the difference.

Through differentiation, you are demonstrating why your customer should do business with you instead of your competitor. If there is no difference, or if the difference is not significant between you and your competitor, your customer has no reason to choose you over the other guy.

Learning to Differentiate

Matt is a radiologist. He has a fairly large practice with a group of other radiologists, and they provide radiology services to several hospitals in their area. Matt and I were visiting recently and I was telling him about this book. He expressed some interest in the value of customer loyalty. My first assumption was that loyalty probably wasn't relevant to his business because people either need his services or they don't. No one stops by for a CAT scan because they like to do business with you.

Matt corrected me and said that his real customers are not his patients, but instead are the physicians who refer patients to him. The problem he disclosed was the difficulty in differentiating his practice from the other radiologists in town. They all use the same equipment. They are all board certified. They are all competent, educated, and similarly equipped. "So how do I represent myself differently?" he asked.

We thought about his situation for a few minutes and then organized our observations.

1. Matt's customers are the referring physicians.
2. Patients go to the radiologist their attending physician recommends.
3. Any action Matt takes should be directed toward the referring physician.
4. There is little perceived difference between one radiologist and another.

Based on these observations, Matt devised a plan to include the referring physician as well as the patient's family physician on the progress of the patient. Whenever a procedure is performed on the patient (an X-ray, CAT scan, or any other treatment) the referring physician is notified immediately by e-mail or fax. This electronic contact is much faster than any courier or regular mail contact. The referring physician can maintain contact with the patient, is able to visit the patient in the hospital, if appropriate, or can schedule follow-up office visits. The referring physician is empowered to oversee his patient. Instead of the patient feeling like they are dealing with several different vendors of healthcare, the patient feels there is a coordinated effort being made in their treatment. For a referring physician, Matt's follow-up e-mails and faxes are powerful differentiators. Matt clearly defines who the customer is and what is of value to them. The referring physicians want to use Matt's group for all their radiology work because there is a meaningful difference.

Some businesses such as Matt's group can successfully differentiate by offering one or two unique services. Other businesses have been successful by offering many unique differentiators. Fresh Market is a small chain of grocery stores in the southeastern part of the country. Fresh Market stores are larger than convenient stores but are substantially smaller than a supermarket. Fresh Markets are differentiated from other grocery stores by their interior design, product offerings, and level of service. Fresh Markets do not compete with supermarkets. The Fresh Market shopping experience is much more sensual. The lighting is more like a lounge than a grocery store. Spotlights illuminate the produce, meat, seafood, and bakery departments. Aisles of canned goods, pasta, and other staples have dimmer lighting. As the name implies, Fresh Markets have a limited selection of everything except fresh meats, fresh produce, fresh bakery goods, candies, coffees, specialty foods, cheeses, and wine. A shopping trip to the Fresh Market is a treat. The Fresh Market is different from other grocery stores. They provide a unique shopping experience and are rewarded with a growing loyal clientele.

If you want to maximize loyalty in your customers, you must also give your customers a differentiator. In your bagel shop, clothing store, insurance agency, law office, medical practice, or whatever kind of business you have, you need to provide a unique difference to give your customers a reason to return.

7 Universal Values

Customers want seven things in every transaction:

1. **Value.** Don't confuse value with price. Price is only one part of value. People buy for convenience, selection, image, and a million other reasons. It's your job to find out which values are most important to each of your customers. Only by understanding and providing the specific value your customer wants can you expect them to be loyal.

2. **Communication.** Customers want complete information and full disclosure about their purchases. People don't want surprises with their purchases. They want straight talk and they appreciate communication on a regular basis. Communication includes everything you say to your customers before, during, and after the sale. It includes what you say as well as how you say it.

3. **Attitude.** Caring, friendliness, and courtesy will never go out of style. The most powerful demonstration of your attitude is your smile. Even if all your business is conducted over the phone, your customers can detect if you are smiling and if you are happy to be doing business with them. Another point about smiling: You can ask almost any question, and if you are smiling, the customer

will detect sincerity and be delighted to answer. A smiling face that asks the question, "Mrs. Jones may I ask how old you are?" is likely to get the right answer, while the same question asked with a non-smiling face is likely to get the answer, "None of your business." Keep in mind that there are many different types of smiles: contrived, warm, weary, inviting, threatening, and understanding to name a few. To smile effectively you must know why you are smiling. When the smile is genuine pleasantness it will convey the right message to your customer.

4. **Reliability.** The product must do what it is supposed to do for as long as the customer expects it to do it. Companies and individuals with the most loyal customers have a history of under-promising and over-delivering reliability. The law of reliability states, "Do what you say you are going to do, when you say you are going to do it." The law is basic, but it is also critical to developing loyal customers.

5. **Quality.** The customer must feel as if they are getting what they are paying for. The term *quality* pertains to both product and transaction. For example, the quality of an insurance company or the insurance policy may not be evident for many years, but the quality of contact the policyholder has with the salesperson or customer service representative must meet the standards he expects. You may not be able to control the product, but you can control the transaction and thereby influence the customers' expectations for quality.

6. **Assurance.** Every customer wants assurance that they are making the best purchase. The customer's family, friends, or coworkers may not be generous with compliments or assurance that the customer made the right purchase, so it is up to you to make sure the customer is assured their purchases are the right ones for them. Customers measure the degree of assurance they are receiving by noting if the people they are doing business with do what they say they're going to do when they say they're going to do it.

7.   **Understanding.** Customers want to be important enough that their wants and needs are understood.

A single differentiator will not answer all the things a customer wants in a transaction, but to be an effective differentiator it must address at least one of the seven. For example, Lou Holtz's greeting, "How can I help you?" is a sincere statement that lets people know he wants to understand them and their wants. He differentiates himself from others by being truly interested in helping people.

During this discussion of differentiation we looked at the seven things a customer wants. Any of the seven can be used as an effective differentiator, however only three of the things customers want actually have an impact on loyalty, beyond being a differentiator.

For example, people appreciate a good attitude, friendly service, and a warm smile, but a good attitude is not, in itself, going to create loyalty. People don't become loyal to a seller because he smiles a lot and is friendly unless the only competition is a bunch of grumpy old men.

The only three "customer wants" that actually create loyalty are value, assurance, and effective communication.

In the next chapter we will discuss value and assurance and in Chapter Six we will cover effective communication.

Summary

✓ People buy what they buy where they buy it because of the value the product or service provides. Do not confuse value with price. Price is only one part of value.

✓ Differentiators make one business, product, or seller distinguishable from another. Differentiators demonstrate why your customers should buy from you. If there is no difference, your customers have no reason to choose you over your competition.

✓ Quality and service have become commodities. When everyone offers terrific quality and great service, these attributes are not differentiators.

✓ You are singular—there is only one of you. When you interact with customers, your unique skills, experiences, and concern are the greatest differentiators.

✓ Twenty percent of the businesses operating today sell 80 percent of all goods and services that are sold. Differentiators account for this disparity of success.

✓ Customers want seven things in every transaction: value, effective communication, a positive attitude, reliability, quality, assurance, and understanding.

✓ The only three "customer wants" that actually create loyalty are value, assurance, and effective communication.

Have you differentiated yourself? Take this test and see.

Differentiation Test

1. Who are you? Make a list and name 10, 20, or 30 things that describe you. Your list should include a description of your attributes, experiences, intellect, and accomplishments.

2. Make a list of 10–30 things that you absolutely positively know. These are your core beliefs. These beliefs are the things that make you different.

3. How does your business, your workday, and interactions with customers reflect your unique knowledge, skills, and attributes?

4. How would your customers describe you?

5. How do you want your customers to describe you?

6. Give specific examples of how you and your business are different from the businesses you compete against.

Chapter 5

Value and Assurance

Value or the worth of something is customer-centric. The customer always decides what is of value to them. Value is determined by the customer's specific tastes, preferences, wants, and needs. I mentioned earlier that we should not confuse value with price: Price is only one component of value. People base their purchasing decisions on their specific situation and desires.

Customers who are buying the identical product may be buying it for different reasons. For example, three shoppers buy the same type of insurance policy from the same company and the same insurance agent. Kevin is 30 years old and his wife is pregnant with their first child. In order to protect his family in the event of his death, he applies for and purchases a $250,000 life insurance policy. He believes the monthly premium is a worthwhile expense for the comfort he receives knowing his family will be able to continue their standard of living. The policy has value to Kevin.

Bob and Joe are partners in a heating and air conditioning company. They owe $250,000 on a building their business occupies. If either of them could not work at the business every day, there would not be enough money to make the mortgage payment. Their attorney suggests that each of them applies for and purchases a $250,000 life insurance policy. In the event that either partner dies before the building is paid off, the remaining partner will have the money to retire the mortgage. Bob and Joe believe the premium they pay is a good value.

Jack is a big basketball fan of his college alma mater. The team has done so well in recent years that tickets to their home games are no longer available. Jack's alumni association offers season tickets to alumni members who will become life members of the association. Life membership to the association requires members to purchase a $250,000 life insurance policy naming the association as beneficiary. Jack applies for and purchases the insurance in order to qualify for season tickets. He believes the premium he pays for the insurance is a good value in exchange for his basketball tickets.

These insurance buyers are finding value in the same product in different ways. Kevin finds value because of the love he has for his family and knowing they will be able to continue their standard of living. Bob and Joe find value for business reasons. Jack finds value because he is trading the cost of insurance for a seat at the basketball games next season.

Even though it is the same product, each customer is applying his or her own definition of value. If you know how to listen carefully, customers are always willing to tell you what they value.

Value Propositions

How a customer perceives the value of your product or service can be described as your *value proposition*. A value proposition goes beyond just a description of the product or service. A value proposition encompasses the true usefulness or specific benefits the product or service provides.

More than seven decades ago a small aircraft company started in Wichita to do what others said couldn't be done: build a monoplane with a full cantilever wing. A full cantilever wing is a single wing airplane without supporting struts or braces. When the Cessna All Purpose took off on August 13, 1927, the aviation world was forever changed. In fact, Clyde Cessna's cantilever design has been the standard ever since. The company has successfully continued operations through all these years embracing innovation, ingenuity, and initiative.

The Cessna 172 is the single most popular airplane ever built. More than 30,000 of these planes have flown since their introduction in 1956. More pilots have learned to fly in a 172 than any other aircraft. Even though the Cessna 172 has evolved substantially over the years, pilots can transition easily from an early 172 to the newest model. Pilots who learned to fly in an old 172 can hop in any of Cessna's newer models and feel comfortable at the controls immediately. Cessna has kept the design simple and very similar to every earlier model.

Every pilot considering the purchase of a single engine airplane is familiar with Cessna's unique value proposition. Cessna 172s have the best safety record; are economical and the easiest to fly and maintain; and offer the ease of transition from old to new models. Cessna competes against other airplane manufacturers that build faster, sleeker, and cheaper aircraft but no competitor can match Cessna's unique value proposition.

A unique value proposition will allow your customers to immediately identify why they should do business with you and arm them with a message to tell other potential customers.

My wife, JoyAnn, and I have leased our car for several years. The value proposition for leasing a car says your monthly payment is less on a leased automobile and you don't have to mess around with selling the vehicle after the lease is over. Another way of expressing the value proposition is that you are only paying for that part of the automobile's life that you are using. Rather than paying $400 a month to build equity and ultimately own a car, we prefer to pay $300 a month and walk away from the car every three years.

Leasing is a good arrangement for us, but an even better arrangement would be to lease from a pool of automobiles. For example, a car or leasing company could offer a choice of automobiles. The pool of lease cars could include convertibles, sedans, and SUVs. Instead of $300 a month perhaps the pool arrangement would cost $450 a month. Every six months participants could turn in their leased car for another car that is in the pool. Leasees could enjoy variety and plan what car they would be using to coincide with vacations or other special times.

I don't know of a company that offers this type of lease but I have mentioned the idea to several friends who are currently leasing their cars. Every one of them expressed an interest in participating. They all felt the value proposition was compelling enough that they would be eager to increase their lease payment by 50 to 100 percent.

The creative possibilities in developing a value proposition are endless. Value propositions are built around what customers value, and this value makes price a secondary consideration.

Many times your customer will place a very high value on only one specific aspect of your product, so that little else matters. There is a dry cleaning business that picks up and delivers to the building where I work. I asked a friend in my building if he used this dry cleaners and, if so, why? He told me he did, and it was because of the convenience of bringing his laundry to work. I asked him if he would be interested in another dry cleaner that charged much less. He told me, "No." How about a cleaner that did a better job? "Not interested," he said. What about faster turn around time I asked? "I don't want to change dry cleaners," he snapped back. This guy was loyal. He continues to use the same dry cleaner every week. He is loyal for one reason: location. His whole value proposition in dealing with this dry cleaner is based solely on the convenience of being able to bring his laundry to work.

A quick look around a convenience store will demonstrate that prices tend to be much higher than at a nearby supermarket. But the name says it all: people shop there because it is convenient. The customer might pay as much as 50 percent more, but it is worth it to the customer to not have to stand in line or search through long aisles for their purchase. The value to the customer is convenience. Customer value is based on convenience, price, image, prestige, largeness, smallness, and every other descriptive word known to man. The key to creating lasting loyalty is the identification of what is of value to each of your customers.

Usually the customer will tell you, but sometimes it can be tricky to determine value. The following two stories illustrate how direct and how elusive determining customer value can be.

The first story illustrates how customers will tell you exactly what they want if you give them a chance. My wife graduated from Purdue and shared this campus legend.

University Lets Students Make Their Own Way

Purdue University is located in West Lafayette, Indiana, in the northwestern part of the state. The main street in West Lafayette that leads to the campus is State Street. The main campus entrance off of State Street leads to an open meadow with a school building on each end. There is a sidewalk leading from one building to the other building through the middle of the meadow. This sidewalk is called "Hello Walk" because students are encouraged to say, "Hello" as they pass each other.

Over the years, additional buildings have been built around the meadow, which is known as Memorial Meadow because John Purdue is now buried there. As new buildings were built, new sidewalks were not immediately added. The new buildings were completed and landscaping was put in place, but there were no sidewalk leading to the buildings. During the new buildings' first year of operation students would find their way in the most convenient manner. Depending on where they were coming from, students would cross the lawn in what appeared a totally random fashion.

After a year of students tracking across the lawn, the campus construction people knew exactly where to build sidewalks. The student paths became student sidewalks. The placement of the sidewalks was exactly right because the students demonstrated where they wanted them. All the discussion groups in the world could not produce better results than letting the students vote with their feet. If you are patient and listen carefully, your customers will tell you exactly what they want.

Tenants Get What They Want

This second story demonstrates how elusive customers can be in helping you determine what they want.

Several years ago in a large office building in a downtown metropolis, the tenants were angry. They were complaining to the building managers that something had to be done about the wait for the elevators.

The building managers were sensitive to the complaints and hired an engineering firm to see what could be done. The engineers explored the possibility of changing the motors on the elevators to make them go faster. This idea didn't work because the entire elevator system would have to be changed, not just the motors. Another idea was to deem some elevators "express elevators," which would only stop at higher floors. A great deal of money was spent on engineering studies, but nothing seemed doable or affordable. Even the possibility of hanging new elevators on the outside of the building was explored.

A solution was finally found that was affordable, ended all the complaints, cost $25,000, and didn't require major modification to the building. Can you guess what the answer was?

Mirrors. Mirrors! Mirrors? A different engineering firm was hired to assess the problem. They came back with a solution in three days and said the solution would cost $25,000. The building managers were delighted with the price but suspicious of the solution. The firm declared the problem was that tenants were complaining about having to wait for an elevator. Every building has tenants who complain about the elevators. The elevators could travel 100 miles per hour and tenants would still complain. The real problem was the tenants' complaints. If you can stop the complaints, isn't that a good sign the solution has been found? The firm lined the lobby walls with mirrors—$25,000 worth of mirrors. Wherever a tenant looked they could see themselves or someone else. People are fascinated with themselves and others. The complaints stopped. The problem wasn't the speed of the elevators, it was boredom. Once the tenants had something to watch, they were happy.

The key was accurately defining what the customers (tenants) wanted. The customers didn't really know the solution, but they did know the problem: They didn't enjoy waiting for an elevator. Sometimes your customer will not be able to accurately define what they want. It's your job to keep asking questions until you can determine what is of value to your customer. It is also important to keep asking questions because in many situations the customer has several values they need satisfied.

The customer's perception of value is the only value that matters. This perception is influenced and affected by every facet of how you deal with customers and how they deal with you.

Frequency of Payment Can Affect Loyalty

The more aware your customers are of the cost of your product or service, the more likely they are to use it. The more your customers use your product or service, the more likely they are to buy it again.

For example, a downtown athletic club offers its members a choice of paying their dues on an annual or monthly basis. The annual cost is $600 and the monthly cost is $50. They do not offer a discount for paying annually or an additional charge for paying monthly. The club finds that its members who pay on a monthly basis are much more likely to renew their memberships. Monthly members are reminded every month of the cost and are more likely to work out more frequently in order to get their money's worth. Members who pay on an annual basis are not reminded of their expense. As months go by, the annual member is less likely to use the health club's facilities to work out. By the end of the year, the annual member isn't working out at all and is unlikely to renew his or her membership. The price is the same but the perception is different.

Magazine subscriptions are usually sold on a one-, two-, or three-year basis. Typically, only 60 percent of the people who subscribe to a magazine renew their subscriptions. The longer the period of subscription, the lower the renewal rates. Publishers spend substantial sums of money in replacing as much as 40 percent of their customers every year.

Daily newspapers usually require their customers to subscribe only on a weekly or monthly basis and every month the customer is sent a bill. This monthly reminder encourages subscribers to read the paper and get their money's worth. Renewal rates are substantially higher for this type publication.

The timing of payment encourages your customers to use your product. The more they use your product or service, the more likely they are to continue doing business with you. Lawyers, dentists, health clubs, or any business that can allow customers to pay for their product or service as they use it will create loyalty.

Ducts Unlimited

Daryl Mirza is the owner of Ducts Unlimited in Chicago. Daryl should receive an award for cleverness in coming up with the name of his business. Ducts Unlimited cleans restaurant hoods and ducts all over Chicagoland. Daryl's employees arrive after a restaurant has closed and go about the dirty job of removing dirt and grease. Because it is after normal business hours, Daryl's employees usually do not see the restaurant owner or anyone from the restaurant while they are on the premises.

Restaurant hoods and ducts need to be cleaned at least several times each year to satisfy insurance requirements. When Daryl started his business more than 16 years ago he placed a small sticker on each hood after it was cleaned. The sticker gave the name of Daryl's company and showed what day the hood was cleaned. Usually hoods get dirty again within just a few days or weeks after they are cleaned. Customers would call to complain that the hood hadn't been thoroughly cleaned and Daryl would send a crew back to the restaurant to touch up the job.

Several years ago, Daryl used the example set by businesses that performed oil changes and began putting the next date when the hood would need to be cleaned, rather than the last date it was cleaned. A remarkable thing happened: Daryl didn't get any more complaints. Oftentimes the next cleaning got moved to an earlier date, giving Ducts Unlimited additional work. Before changing the date on the stickers, Daryl always seemed to be competing with other businesses doing similar work. Now Daryl's customers don't look at the hood and think it wasn't cleaned properly. Instead they feel Ducts Unlimited is fully aware of the condition of their hood and the next cleaning is already scheduled. Daryl changed his customers perception of value simply by changing the date.

Asking sincere questions is the key to determining what is of value to your customer. Your ability to learn what your customer's value is your most important challenge. It doesn't matter if you have a terrific product or service. The only thing that matters is "the value to the customer."

A substantial amount of time and money is spent on training salespeople in product knowledge. Product knowledge is very important, but not nearly as important as customer knowledge. Product knowledge is important only so you can know how to help your customer.

The purpose of every product and service is to solve a problem or fill a need. This is where the questioning begins. "How can I help you?" "What are you working on?" "Where will you be wearing the new dress?" "What kind of project are you involved in?" "What have you used before?" Definition of a need or a problem is the start of knowing and understanding your customer. Offering a product for sale or demonstrating a product without going through this step will end any chance you might have of knowing and understanding your customer. The customer will intuitively understand that you're interested in selling something more than you are interested in helping them.

There are two kinds of dollars: absolute dollars and relative dollars. Absolute dollars express the price of something in dollars. For example, a gallon of gasoline costs $1.50 or a head of lettuce costs $1.

Relative dollars express the price of something with added value. For example, I own a small powerboat. I park my boat and buy gasoline at a marina that is on the water. I can buy gasoline at a local gas station for about 40 percent less than it costs at the marina. However, I don't feel the savings begins to offset the inconvenience, danger, and mess of hauling a gas can around in my automobile. The added value of convenience, safety, and cleanliness is worth more to me than the cost difference. I use relative dollars to buy gasoline at the marina.

The grocery store where I shop offers various kinds of lettuce for about $1 a pound. They also offer a lettuce mix, which is displayed in a plastic-lined box next to the loose lettuce. The mixed lettuce is a variety of several different kinds of lettuce that is washed, cut up, and ready to eat. This lettuce mix costs around $6 a pound. Guess which one I buy? I buy the more expensive kind. Why? I like the variety. I don't have to buy 10 pounds of lettuce in order to have a selection and there is no waste. The key statement here is "and there is no waste." People make emotional decisions for logical reasons. The tag line of "there is no waste" makes the emotional decision to "buy what you want" logical. The logic of "I'm not wasteful" justifies the additional expense. We aren't doing any sophisticated double-entry accounting. We are simply justifying our lettuce expenditure of $6 a pound versus

$1 a pound. There is nothing wrong with this. All of us can buy whatever we can afford, but we must justify why we do it. Value statements such as, "We like the variety and there is no waste," makes the additional expense logical.

This justification is important in demonstrating value. We should always talk about value rather than price. When we deal with our customers, we should place value first because that is why the customer is doing business with us. Value is why the customer comes back over and over again, demonstrating loyalty.

It's important that we talk about what our product or service does—what its value is—rather than just how much it cost.

Remember George the car salesman we discussed in Chapter 3? George never talked about the competition. When George said, "Toyota applies four coats of paint." I never knew if the competition was applying three coats or five coats. George was selling what he had to sell: four coats of paint. The man at the marina never mentions the price of gas in town, he only says, "Do you want me to fill it up?" He is inferring, "rather than you carrying a leaky old gas can around in your car."

Value is all about finding what is important to your customers and making sure they receive what is important to them in every transaction.

Masters of Value

Dentists have become masters at providing value. While some may believe that all dentists are the same, most recognize all dentists' offices are not created equally. Many dentists' offices feature full-length motion pictures and stereophonic music of the patient's choice. I haven't seen a dentists' office equipped with a Sony PlayStation 2, but if it is going to happen, it will happen first in a dentists' office.

I am not suggesting that healthcare providers or other businesses turn their waiting rooms into entertainment centers, but I am suggesting that you think beyond just your product or service when you attempt to provide value.

Inventions

I like to think of myself as being inventive. I don't really invent anything; I just come up with ideas for what should be invented. When I was 12 years old I lived with my family in Birmingham, Alabama. The Birmingham newspaper ran a weekly article that encouraged readers to send in their ideas for inventions. If your idea was published, you would receive a prize of $5. I received the prize several times for my inventions. My best invention was "soft butter." I suggested that butter and air could be mixed together to produce butter that was soft and wouldn't tear up toast, muffins, or whatever else you were spreading the butter on. Feel free to repeat this item of interest at any upcoming cocktail parties you may be attending. Right after someone mentions they are purchasing a new BMW you can say, "That's nothing. I know the guy that invented soft butter."

More recently I have come up with more high-tech inventions. My current idea involves motion pictures. Remember the movie *Forrest Gump*? Remember the part of the movie when Forrest is inserted into the scene of President Kennedy's inauguration? Another example of this technology are the TV specials where the magician David Copperfield has a discussion with Orson Wells. How do they do that? Filmmakers have the ability to digitize images and add or delete those images on the big screen. My idea is to digitize all the actors. Then we could go to Blockbuster and order movies with our favorite actors. For example, I'd like to rent the great movie classic *The African Queen* and instead of Humphrey Bogart and Katharine Hepburn I'd like Tom Cruise and Jennifer Lopez to play the parts of Charlie Allnut and Rose Sayer. This method would cause a great boom for the movie rental business. They could rent the same movie over and over again but with different actors each time.

When I told my son Matthew about my invention, he suggested ice cream that is room temperature. This special ice cream would have the same texture, firmness, and flavor of regular ice cream, but it would be room temperature. You would never get an ice cream headache and it wouldn't melt.

The point of these playful ideas is to look at the possibilities in your business. You may not be able to invent new products or even reinvent your product, but by reassessing your value proposition you can make a dramatic difference in how your customers view what you offer. Your ability to creatively produce a value proposition, live by it, and announce it to your customers is key to successfully creating loyalty.

More Ice Cream

In my hometown there are two ice cream shops that are located directly across the street from each other. Both of these businesses are individually owned and are not part of a chain or franchise. Their signs proclaim "Homemade ice cream." They are about the same size and from what I can tell as a causal observer they seem to be doing about the same amount of business. I draw this conclusion based on the fact that I have been in both of these enterprises as a customer.

I live in a resort area, and our population increases substantially in the winter months. Because our summers are hot and our winters are warm, ice cream is popular year-round. Locals simply call December through March "season." During season, one of the ice cream shops consistently seems to do more business than its competitor across the street. I haven't conducted any kind of scientific study, but the parking lot in front of one shop is always full. Even during season the one ice cream shop has only a few patrons while the other shop has a long line of folks waiting. I think both shops offer an excellent product and both shops are equally clean and well equipped, but one shop is doing five or six times as much business.

Considering my passion for customer loyalty, you might well imagine my curiosity and interest in figuring out why one ice cream shop sells so much more than the other. While there is no apparent difference in these two businesses, I have learned there is a huge difference in how they do business.

The more popular ice cream shop participates in school outings and events. When the local grammar school has a fair, concert, or any kind of special event, only one of these two businesses supplies ice cream. When a local high school takes a field trip, guess who supplies the ice cream? Only one of these businesses host monthly coloring contests for pre-school children. (Covering their walls with all the artwork for parents and grandparents to come and see.) The more successful ice cream shop has a value proposition that screams "We are part of the community. You know us. We know your kids. We care about you."

Your auto parts business, hobby shop, real estate office, title insurance agency, or dress shop can be reinvented by creatively reassessing or establishing your value proposition.

A final thought about value. The customer always, always, always gets to decide what is of value. Let your customers tell you what is of value and then build and live by a value proposition that serves them.

This Farmer Gives Value

Simon Huber migrated from Germany in 1843 and settled in Starlight, Indiana. He brought with him apple tree saplings ready to plant. The seventh generation of Hubers now lives in Starlight.

In 1926, Joe Huber, Sr. (fourth generation) and his wife, Mary, purchased what is now the Joe Huber Family Farm. They became proud parents of 11 children while they raised cattle and chickens. Mary dressed the chickens as needed for lunch and dinner and the boys milked the cows daily. Back then, many of the farmhands resided at the farmhouse with the rest of the family during harvest.

Joe Huber, Jr., and his wife, Bonnie, lived just up the road from the farm with their five young children and continued to help Joe, Sr., and Mary with the farm while Joe, Jr., worked at the Indiana Gas Company. When Joe, Sr., passed away in 1967, Joe, Jr., and Bonnie purchased the 200-acre farm and moved into the farmhouse. Joe quit his job to become a full-time farmer.

One hot summer day in July 1976, the Hubers had a field full of green beans they were not able to pick in time. Joe said, "Bonnie, what do you think would happen if we put an ad in the newspaper to tell people they can come right to the farm and pick their own green beans?"

People came to the farm in carloads to pick-their-own while Joe, Bonnie, and the children looked at each other in bewilderment. It was difficult to believe that these "city people" thought that picking fruits and vegetables was fun. The garage next to the farmhouse was transformed into a market and soon afterward a new Farm Market Building was constructed.

The Huber family had a whole new variety of "farmhands" that drove out from the city and paid to pick their own produce. It wasn't long before the new farmhands started complaining that they were hungry after picking. Bonnie responded by preparing food in her own kitchen and delivering to her regulars in the Farm Market. Soon afterward, a new restaurant was constructed. Today, Huber Family Farm celebrates spring with a Strawberry Festival, Halloween with a haunted haystack, Christmas with cut-your-own Christmas tree, and every day with hayrides.

Joe and Bonnie started with little belief that people from the city would want to pick their own produce; however, they have built a very substantial business by recognizing what their customers value. If they had listened to the experts, they would have never placed that first newspaper ad. Listening and learning from your customers and understanding what your customers value and delivering that value is a key principle in building loyalty.

Feeling Good

This is a discussion of value. As I mentioned earlier, "the purpose of every product or service is to solve a problem or fill a need." More importantly, the bottom line on any product or service is that it should make the customer feel good. Feeling good is the object of every purchase whether it is a product or a service. Providing value to the customer ultimately makes them feel good.

Assurance

When your customers return to do business with you again and again, they are demonstrating loyalty. The size of their initial purchase doesn't determine loyalty. The level of satisfaction with their initial purchase does not demonstrate loyalty. It is only when they return to buy from you a second, third, or fourth time that they are demonstrating loyalty. The only incentive they have to do business with you on a repeat basis is the assurance you give them that their next purchase will provide as good a value as the last purchase. Assurance is the attraction to return. If a customer doesn't think they will receive the same value on repeat transactions, they have no incentive to return.

Some businesses, such as Office Depot, print the amount the customer has saved by doing business with them on every receipt.

For example, a ream of paper, a box of pencils, and a three-hole punch may cost $15 at Office Depot. The receipt might say, "These same purchases would have cost $17 at a competitor's store. You have saved $2." Office Depot is demonstrating value and the assurance that they will continue to deliver a cost advantage.

A One-Time Deal

My friends Gary and Sharon, recently traveled to Barbados. They purchased an all-inclusive vacation package at a fraction of its regular price. Tourism in Barbados, as many places, has continued to suffer since the September 11, 2001, terrorist attacks. Gary and Sharon flew to Barbados and stayed at a first-class hotel-resort for less than half of the normal rate. They received a terrific value. When they returned they said it was the best vacation of their lives. I asked Gary if they would go back again next year. He told me, "Probably not. We'd never be able to get the same deal. It was a one-time special."

Value and assurance are linked together. A great value is only a one-time deal unless it is accompanied by an assurance. Assuring your customers that your value proposition is a constant gives them the confidence to return to buy from you again and again.

Knowing What to Expect

McDonald's and Denny's restaurants enjoy a loyal clientele. These restaurants have been successful because they consistently meet their customer's expectations. Few people claim they have never tasted a hamburger better than McDonald's. Few people say the best steak they ever ate was at Denny's. Yet both of these restaurant chains see their customers come back on a regular basis. The reason for this loyalty is because the customer's expectations are met. The customers know what to expect. Every trip to a McDonald's or Denny's assures the customer of his or her expectation. Customers know these restaurants. They receive the same value time and time again. The customer is confident he or she will receive full value.

Interactions where the customer's expectations are met are reassuring to the customer. The more times it happens, the more assured the customer is that it will continue.

80-Percent Failure Rate

A few months ago I attended a meeting with the CEO of a major American company. He told the audience that he had seen a recent report that claimed 80 percent of the things salespeople promise their customers they do not deliver. The salesman says, "I'll call you back." But he doesn't call back. "I'll get that report to you." But he doesn't send the report. "I'll schedule a meeting." But he doesn't schedule a meeting. "I'll get shipping to give you a call." But shipping never calls. These are just a few examples of the many things salespeople promise and don't deliver. I don't know if the 80-percent figure is accurate, but I do know this behavior does not earn loyalty. Everything you say to your customers is an assurance. When you don't do the things you say you will do, you negate the value of your product or service.

Keep in mind that we are talking about what you can do to create customer loyalty, not what the marketing department or the production department or someone else in the company can do. What you can do is whatever you say you will do. Doing what you say you will do when you say you will do it is the best way to assure your customers they should continue doing business with you. When you promise to call the customer back in an hour, you are building the customer's expectation and creating an opportunity to assure the customer. When you promise to ship the material no later than tomorrow, you are building the customer's expectation and creating an opportunity to assure the customer. Every time you make a promise and then fulfill the promise, you are building a stronger bond with the customer. Eventually, the customer believes you will fulfill every promise you make. This assurance you have given confirms to the customer that they are making the right decision in doing business with you. The customer will want to return to you on a repeat basis, and you have empowered the customer to refer business to you. The more promises you make, the more opportunities you have to build customer loyalty. The words do not need to be, "I promise to call you back in an hour." You can simply say, "I'll get back to you in an hour." The important part is calling the customer back. Even if you call to say you do not have the information but you are still working on the customer's request, calling the customer within the hour builds assurance. It builds confidence in the customer that you will always do what you say you'll do when you say you'll do it.

Assurance is making promises and keeping them. Assurance is always being accountable to your customers. Offering assurance and being accountable to your customers provokes an emotional response from your customers. People make emotional decisions for logical reasons, and one of the most logical reasons for your customer to do business with you is that you are accountable and do what you say you will do.

"It Works or We'll Fix It Free"

The Zippo Manufacturing Company has produced 300 million windproof lighters since 1932. Every Zippo lighter is backed by its famous guarantee: "It works or we fix it free." Zippo's literature says, "Any Zippo lighter, when returned to our factory, will be put in first-class mechanical condition free of charge, for we have yet to charge a cent for the repair of a Zippo lighter, regardless of age or condition." Zippo is assuring its customers that any Zippo lighter will always perform the same as the day it was purchased.

Today, Zippo windproof lighters represent one of the fastest-growing categories in the world of collectibles. These lighters are bought, sold, and traded by thousands of enthusiastic fans from every continent. Zippo regularly introduces new lighters commemorating everything from Corvettes to past U.S. presidents and their loyal customers continue to buy new Zippo lighters every year.

Zippo enjoys the emotional attachment many of their customers have for their product. Their customers recall carrying a Zippo lighter overseas while they were in the service or other memorable times in their lives. They remember the guarantee. They remember the lighter always faithfully producing a flame. Despite the decline in cigarette smoking, the Zippo Company sells to more than 4 million loyal customer collectors. Their assurance of value carries over to their entire product line including tape measures, knives, and writing instruments.

Swiss Army knives and Gibson guitars are two other examples of products that enjoy fierce loyalty. These manufacturers continually assure their customers of the value their products provide. Their value propositions are woven into every aspect of their products and services. The value propositions of these products are so compelling that customers buy them as collectibles even when they have no utilitarian use of them.

My friend Doug is an executive with a large company. Doug was in California at a business convention and heard a marketing executive from the Harley Davidson Motorcycle Company give a speech. In the speech he discussed the tremendous loyalty Harley Davidson has created. The marketing executive mentioned that many of their customers even tattoo the Harley Davidson logo on their bodies. "Now that's loyalty!" he commented.

When Doug returned home from his business trip he visited the local Harley Davidson dealership. Doug said that when he arrived at the dealership wearing a suit and tie he could hear snickers of "Rolex rider." Doug was impressed with the quality and glamour of the big motorcycles and purchased a Harley Davidson Road King for nearly $20,000.

Doug researched motorcycles further and discovered that BMW builds an equally impressive motorcycle that offers a much smoother ride. Doug became the proud owner of a second motorcycle. Despite the rough ride, he didn't sell or trade in his Harley. The value and assurance Harley Davidson gives for every one of their motorcycles makes Doug confident his investment in a Harley will always be solid.

Asking for Assurance

Consider some of the people you do business with: your real estate sales agent, your insurance agent, your jeweler, your doctor, your stockbroker, and others. Are you still shopping to find one of these people? If you find a better price or a better product, do you investigate further or report your findings to your current supplier? If you report your findings to your current supplier, you are asking for assurance. If you are asking for assurance, you are testing the confidence you have in your current supplier. None of us knows enough about everything to be our own expert: We depend on other professionals. Customers do repeat business with their current supplier because they are continually assured that they will get what they expect. It's not the best price or the absolute best product. There is always a lower price or a more spectacular product. Assurance that the customer will feel good about their purchase and will always have their expectations met is a critical principle of creating loyal customers.

"Oh What a Relief It Is"

Many companies use slogans in their advertisements. These slogans are clever one- or two-line statements about the company's product or service. Companies spend substantial sums of money in advertising and promoting their slogans in hopes that it will capture the attention of their customers. The development and use of slogans is very subjective; however, slogans that capture a company's value proposition and give assurance are the most effective.

In 1976, Alka Seltzer introduced the slogan "Plop, plop, fizz, fizz. Oh what a relief it is." Alka Seltzer's value proposition is clear: "Plop, plop, fizz, fizz" is descriptive and "Oh what a relief it is" gives assurance that you will find relief with the product.

In late 2002, United Parcel Service (UPS) introduced its slogan "We've got brown." This slogan offers neither a value proposition nor assurance. Contrast UPS's slogan to their competitor Federal Express's "When it absolutely, positively has to be there overnight." Federal Express demonstrates a clear value proposition and uses adjectives to assure the customer so there is no doubt Federal Express will deliver.

Some slogans are immediately recognizable and attributable to a company, but still don't offer value or assurance. In 1988, Nike introduced "Just do it." Nike has spent enormous sums of money on making sure everyone in the world will think of Nike when they hear, "Just do it." Everyone does think of Nike when they hear the slogan, but the slogan offers no value or assurance. The same problem is true of Toshiba's slogan "Hello Tosh, gotta Toshiba?" which was introduced in 1984.

Try to match the following list of slogans with the companies they represent. There is a list of these companies listed with their slogans and the year the slogan was introduced at the end of this chapter.

Slogans

"Mm mm good."
"Look Ma no cavities."
"Let your fingers do the walking."

"Be all that you can be."

"Fly the friendly skies."

"All the news that's fit to print."

"It takes a licking and keeps on ticking."

"The uncola."

"It takes a tough man to make a tender chicken."

"Good to the last drop."

"Got milk?"

"When it rains it pours."

"The ultimate driving machine."

"The antidote for civilization."

"Finger lickin good."

"Say it with flowers."

"Nothing runs like a deere."

Companies

BMW

Campbell's Soup

Club Med

Crest

FTD

John Deere

Kentucky Fried Chicken

Maxwell House

Milk

Morton Salt

Perdue

7-Up

The New York Times

Timex

United Airlines

U.S. Army

Yellow Pages

The purpose of this exercise is to give you examples to help you distill your own value proposition and assurance into one or two sentences. When you consolidate your value and assurance into a concise statement, your customer can do the same. When someone tells a friend about Federal Express by saying, "When it absolutely, positively has to be there overnight," they have communicated value and assurance. A slogan helps your customers understand the value and assurance of your product or service and gives them the words to share with others. Equally important, your statement of value and assurance becomes a mantra for you and the people you work with.

This exercise of describing value and assurance will work just as well for you if you are a corporate employee, business professional, or a lone practitioner. Your customers, whether they are internal or external, want to receive value and assurance. If you want to create loyalty, it is your responsibility to deliver value and assurance. You are the business to your customers.

You may be buried deep in the IT department, but you will create a bond of loyalty if you consistently deliver value and assurance to your internal customers. When you are known for accuracy or timeliness and you back this value up with a consistent history, your internal customers become loyal to you.

You may be only one salesperson for a large furniture store or design studio, but your ability to provide value and assurance will create loyalty in your customers. Your store's or studio's value proposition might be a superior selection. Your value proposition might be knowledge of your customer's specific tastes.

Summary

✓ Value, or the worth of something, is customer-centric. The customer always decides what is of value to them. Customers buying identical products may be buying it for different reasons.

✓ If you listen carefully, customers are always willing to tell you what they value. Let your customer tell you what they value and then build and live by a value proposition that serves your customers.

✓ How a customer perceives the value of your product or service can be described as your value proposition. A unique value proposition will allow your customers to immediately identify why they should do business with you and arm them with a message to tell other potential customers.

✓ The more aware your customers are of the cost of your product, the more likely they are to use it. The more your customers use your product, the more likely they are to buy it again.

✓ The purpose of every product is to solve a problem or fill a need. Ultimately, the outcome of every transaction should be to make the customer feel good.

✓ The only incentive your customers have to do business with you on a repeat basis is the assurance you give them that their next purchase will provide as good a value as the last. Assurance is the attraction to return.

Answers to slogan quiz:

Yellow Pages	"Let your fingers do the walking." (1964)
United Airlines	"Fly the friendly skies." (1966)
U.S. Army	"Be all that you can be." (1981)
The New York Times	"All the news that's fit to print." (1896)
7-Up	"The uncola." (1973)
Timex	"It takes a licking and keeps on ticking." (1956)
Kentucky Fried Chicken	"Finger lickin good." (1962)
Milk	"Got milk?" (1993)
Campbell's Soup	"Mm mm good." (1935)
John Deere	"Nothing runs like a deere." (1972)
Morton Salt	"When it rains it pours." (1911)
Crest	"Look Ma no cavities" (1958)
Perdue	"It takes a tough man to make a tender chicken." (1972)

Maxwell House	"Good to the last drop." (1915)
BMW	"The ultimate driving machine." (1975)
Club Med	"The antidote for civilization." (1982)
FTD	"Say it with flowers." (1917)

Chapter 6

Effective Communication

Once a human being arrives on this earth, communication is the largest single factor determining what kinds of relationships he makes with others and what happens to him in the world about him.

—Virginia Satir, pioneer in the field of family therapy

Hundreds of books have been written on effective communication. These books talk about power phrases, body language, communicating through how you dress, presentation techniques, gender-specific tactics, and a host of other methods to improve communications. I am sure any of these books will help you in crafting a sales presentation or a speech; however, the book you are holding in your hands is not a book about sales techniques or speech-making skills. This book tells the story of how to get your customers to come back to do business with you again and again. We will discuss a few specific techniques, but the real importance of this information is to share the principle of effective communication as a means of creating loyalty.

We communicate by what we say, how we say it, and how we look. Social scientists tell us that we judge people 7 percent by what they say, 38 percent on how they say it, and a whopping 55 percent on their appearance. These numbers indicate that the most important part of influencing people is appearance. The numbers are true however keep in mind this is how we judge people when we don't have any other information to base our judgment on.

When you visit a doctor's office for the first time, you already have a preformed judgment of the physician. Even if you weren't referred, you enter the doctor's office with the belief he is educated, knowledgeable, qualified, and able to help you. If the doctor shows up in a crumpled shirt and with little to say, you still hold him in high esteem because of your prejudgment. I am not trying to diminish the value of looking good, speaking well, and having something interesting to say. I want you to understand that relationships are built on deeper information.

Have you ever watched Peter Falk's portrayal of the television detective Columbo? If you have watched the show, then you know that a person can smell like a cigar, dress sloppily, and be vague in their speech, yet still be engaging, endearing, and quite likable. First impressions are important but they are still only first impressions. Our purpose in pursuing a discussion of effective communication is to create a lasting relationship. Our discussion is about your second, third, and fourth impressions.

Effective communication is not a parlor trick or something that only a well-trained orator can accomplish. Flawless elocution is an admirable trait but it isn't necessary to communicate effectively. Communication is effective when it is two-way communication. Effective communication is a combination of reactionary interpersonal skills. Speaking, listening, and learning are the basis for effective communication.

The message you give to your customers and how you deliver that message is central in the process of creating customer loyalty. We will be discussing some specific techniques as examples of how best to communicate with your customers. More important than these specific techniques is that you have a strategy for how you will effectively communicate with your customers.

Customers want straight talk. They want truthful, honest information. An eloquent spin on your product or service may capture their attention, but ultimately, customers want down-to-earth, straight talk. Sales people have been carefully taught to "Sell the sizzle, not the steak." If you only have one steak to sell, that may be fine, but this discussion is about selling many steaks over a long and lasting relationship. Loyal customers are more interested in a meaningful value proposition with real assurances, not a one-time deal.

Both internal and external customers are directed by how you communicate. Sincere, effective communication builds consensus and leads the customer. Consensus builds relationships and loyalty is a relationship. It is the relationship you have with your customers that makes them come back again and again to do business with you.

Have you ever heard the expression "Familiarity breeds contempt"? Do you believe familiarity breeds contempt? Professional familiarity does not breed contempt, it builds relationships. When you demonstrate to your customers that you know and understand them they will respond with loyalty. Customers have contempt when you fail to demonstrate that you recognize their wants, needs, and desires.

In this chapter, we are going to discuss three stages of communication that build relationships:
1. Before we talk.
2. When we talk.
3. After we talk.

Before We Talk

A relationship must exist before you can effectively communicate with your customer. Consider every transaction you have with a customer to be a specific mission: Having a customer buy a product is a mission. Providing customer service is a mission. Setting an appointment is a specific mission. In order for your customers or anyone else to complete a mission, they have to recognize, understand, and agree to a relationship.

Have you ever been in a store and approached someone to ask a question? You think the person whom you are asking a question is a clerk in the store. That person acts indignant and informs you, "I don't work here." She may know the answer to your question, but she is compelled to tell you, "I don't work here." The indignant customer tells you she doesn't work here in order to establish the relationship. Now that you know the person doesn't work at that store, you are also uncomfortable because a relationship didn't exist when you asked the question. Without a relationship in place, both of you feel a sense of anxiety.

The same people, the same store, the same situation, but with different words: "I know you don't work here, but could you me tell where the bakery department is?" Put your mind in this situation. Do you notice a difference? Doesn't this exchange have a different feel? The difference is because a relationship exists. Now both parties feel comfortable and can complete, or attempt to complete, the mission of figuring out where the bakery department is located.

Have you ever received a call like this from a telemarketer? "Hello, Mrs. Jones. This is Bob from the Acme Phone Company. How are you today?" Your immediate thought is, *Bob has a lot of nerve asking me how I am. He doesn't know me from a load of coal. He doesn't care how I am. He doesn't have a right to ask me how I am.* The problem here is that no relationship exists. Here is the same scenario with the same people, same mission, but different words: "Hello, Mrs. Jones. This is Bob from the Acme Phone Company. You don't know me. I know you were not expecting my call. You are not currently a customer of the Acme Phone Company. The purpose of my call is to schedule a time later this week to visit over the phone to discuss some of the advantages Acme offers our customers." These words establish a relationship. The words, "You don't know me. I know you were not expecting my call. You are not currently a customer of Acme Phone company," establishes a relationship. Now you can move ahead with the mission of making an appointment. There isn't a sense of anxiety. The prospect may not agree to an appointment, but you will at least have a relationship from which you can discuss an appointment. Before establishing a relationship, you would have only received an, "I'm not interested," unless the prospect was already set on buying something from the Acme Phone Company.

Before any mission can be undertaken, a relationship must first exist. Creation or explanation of the relationship is the first step in completing any mission with your prospects or clients.

This principle of establishing a relationship is just as important in situations where you are dealing with an existing client or customer.

Ken Bentley was a leading producer in the life insurance business for many years. Ken had a spectacular career and sold life insurance to many well-known people, including Muhammad Ali and Dick Van Dyke.

Ken understood and used the concept of establishing and confirming a relationship in all of his sales interviews. Even with existing clients that he had been dealing with for years, Ken would start each sales interview with a review of the relationship.

Ken kept detailed records of all transactions he had with his clients. In many cases where the client had a more public life, Ken kept a scrapbook of newspaper articles about his client. Before he ever reviewed current policies or talked about new life insurance, Ken would open the scrapbook or other records and revisit the relationship he shared with his client. Before he would undertake any new mission, Ken would make sure the client was reminded of the existing relationship. Any talk of new insurance only came after Ken reinforced his identity as the client's insurance agent. This confirmation of the relationship made the sales of new insurance an easy mission.

The technique of establishing or reestablishing a relationship works equally well with both new prospects and existing customers when you want to complete a mission.

When We Talk

Once a relationship is in place you can attempt to effectively communicate the completion of some mission such as selling, servicing, or educating your customer. Many times, salespeople and account managers call an existing customer and begin the conversation with, "How are you doing today?" This is certainly pleasant enough but it really doesn't do anything to develop loyalty in your customer. Remember, the four things people want in every relationship are:

1. Know me.
2. Understand me.
3. Help me.
4. Lead me.

You have an opportunity to fulfill these four things your customers want in every relationship through your effective communication.

The beginning of a phone call or the initial greeting when you meet with your customer is a great opportunity to send a message of knowing, understanding, helping, and leading. Instead of, "Mr. Jones, this is Bob with The Ace Realty Company. How are you doing today?" try, "Mr. Jones, this is Bob with Ace Realty. I have a home listed for sale in your neighborhood. I'm calling to ask you if you would like to participate in choosing your next neighbor." At this point you can ask Mr. Jones how he is doing, but you won't need to. Mr. Jones will be more interested in your message than reporting on how he feels today. This technique works just as well or better with customers whom you have a long-term relationship with. This is a way of demonstrating you want to help and lead your customer.

For example, you have done business with Joe. You have even socialized with Joe. Joe's kids go to the same school as your kids. You give Joe a call and say, "Joe this is Bob with Tip Top Insurance. How are you doing today?" The conversation then moves to social chit-chat. Joe doesn't have a clue why you called except to maybe shoot the breeze while he is trying to work. He's happy to hear from you, but if he gets another call, Joe will probably put you on hold.

Here is an example with the same people, same relationship, but different words: "Joe, this is Bob with Tip Top. When I got to the office this morning I received some information I need to share with you. Can I see you today?" When you are demonstrating your desire to help and lead your client, whether it is an existing client or not, you are creating and encouraging loyalty.

Another way of demonstrating your desire to give the customer what he wants is to lead in communication. This technique is particularly useful when a customer has a complaint or has an objection to your sales effort.

For example, my mother is a habitual returner. She buys stuff and then brings it back to the store for a refund. I am sure this is an expression of our most fundamental nature of being hunters and gathers. She is really more interested in buying than she is in keeping.

Mom's favorite store is Wal-Mart because of the selection, price, and convenience. But she likes Wal-Mart mostly because of their liberal return policy. It is not unusual for my mother to purchase two or three shirts and then return one or two of them. After she has taken her purchases home, she decides she likes one shirt the best. She puts the two shirts she wants to return back in the blue, plastic Wal-Mart shopping bag and heads back to the store. She walks up to the service counter and the clerk asks, "Can I help you?"

Mom says, "I want to return these shirts."

The clerk asks, "Is there anything wrong with them?"

"I decided I didn't like them," Mom reports.

There is a silent pause as the clerk rifles through the shopping bag. The clerk inspects the shirt as if she might be able to discern why my mother wouldn't like such fine merchandise. I suspect she is also inspecting the shirts to make sure there is no damage or foul play.

Finally, the clerk says, "Okay. Do you want cash or a credit on your charge card?"

Mom takes the cash and splits, only to come back again another day as either a shopper or a returner.

Try this scenario instead:

The clerk asks, "Can I help you?"

Mom says, "I want to return these shirts."

The clerk says, "You want to return these shirts." The clerk makes this a statement not a question. This removes any confrontation from the transaction and demonstrates the clerk knows what the customer wants. This is a confirming statement because it confirms what the customer already knows.

The clerk further confirms the customer's desire by saying, "We handle returns at this counter." This additional confirmation is important because it tells the customer that the clerk understands, everything is going fine, and the customer is being served.

The clerk takes the shirts out of the bag and says, "A lot of people recognize the value of our return policy." It doesn't matter so much what the exact words are. It is just important that the clerk makes a statement that describes the transaction as being common or regular. By making this statement, the clerk is making the customer's concerns or request normal.

By saying, "You want to return these shirts. We handle returns at this counter. A lot of people recognize the value of our return policy," the clerk is showing that she understands what the customer wants and is normalizing the transaction. Now comes the best part. The customer is now receptive to the clerk's leadership because the customer has received confirmation and normalization. The clerk can suggest, "Would you like to see this shirt in a different color, a different size, or would you like to shop for a while to use the credit from the purchases you are returning?"

The steps were confirmation, confirmation, normalization, and lead. "You want to return these shirts," is a confirmation. "We handle returns at this counter," is another confirming statement. "A lot of people recognize the value of our return policy," is a normalizing statement. "Would you like to see this shirt in a different color, or would you like to shop for a while to use the credit from the purchases you are returning?" is a leading suggestion and demonstrates the clerk's leadership. If the Wal-Mart service counter clerk used this confirm, confirm, normalize, and lead technique, more often than not, my mom would choose one of the options offered by the clerk and once again become a Wal-Mart shopper rather than a returner. Your customers will do the same thing. Remember the whole point of customer loyalty is to have your customers buy from you on a repeat basis.

At first, the confirm, confirm, normalize, and lead technique may sound unnatural. It may sound like a sales gimmick or a condescending remark. Actually, it can be very natural. For example, consider your son or nephew or the next-door neighbors' kid falls off his bicycle and cuts his knee. The natural thing for you to say would be, "Awww, you fell off your bike. You cut your knee. Everyone falls when they first learn to ride. You're going to be okay." This is a confirm, confirm, normalize, and lead statement. You probably use it all the time. If you use it with your customers, you will be developing loyalty because it will lead your customers. Customers like to be served by being led if you do it right.

Another example: You have closed the deal on a real estate transaction. A day later your customer announces, "We have thought it over and have decided to hold off on buying right now."

You respond, "You have been thinking about the new home. You have decided to hold off on buying right now. Many people have second thoughts about such a large purchase."

At this point you have confirmed the buyers' positions and have normalized their concerns. They are receptive to what you have to say instead of only repeating their original statement, "We have thought it over and have decided to hold off on buying right now."

They feel their fear and hesitation is natural and they are looking to you for leadership.

You lead, "The home is a wonderful buy. The current interest rate makes it even more attractive. A lot of folks get uncomfortable as they approach a big investment. Can we meet and look at the home again?" Comforted by your words, the customer is more likely than not to act on your leadership and revisit the property. In this situation, the technique of confirm, confirm, normalize, and lead gives you an additional opportunity to assure the customer he or she is making the right decision.

A friend of mine who is in the consulting business told me a story about how she used confirm, confirm, normalize, and lead. She said a client had requested a meeting in their Chicago office with one of her consultants and a group of people from the client-company. The client-company flew several of their top people in from remote locations to attend the meeting. Unfortunately, her consultant didn't show up. The consultant failed to schedule the meeting on her calendar and was a complete no-show. The client had spent a substantial amount of money, disrupted several schedules, and the meeting never happened.

When my friend called the client a few weeks later, after things had cooled down, the client was still angry. The client said they never wanted to do business with the consultants again. My friend replied, "Our consultant didn't show up. Your people had traveled a great distance for nothing and I cannot change what has taken place. At one time the Japanese were our greatest enemy. Today the Japanese are our greatest trade partners. Will you give me another opportunity to work with you?" She didn't get the okay that day but confirm, confirm, normalize, and lead did get her back in the door and they did do business at a later time.

This confirm, confirm, normalize, and lead technique can be used in any situation where the customer has a complaint or objection. Your customer will understand that you are not making excuses. You are not minimizing their complaint and you fully recognize their concerns

By confirming, normalizing, and leading you are communicating to your customers that they are important and you understand them.

Earlier in this chapter I mentioned that the specific words or techniques that we use are not nearly as important as the strategy we employ. Your strategy when you are talking to your customers is to demonstrate a sincere interest in knowing, understanding, helping, and leading. It is this sincere interest that separates you from your competitors.

Knowing, understanding, helping, and leading are linked together. You can't help or lead someone unless you know what they want. When you know the customer and understand how your product or service can benefit them, you are in a position to help and lead them.

Knowing is a description of recognizing the customer's specific desires, wants, and needs as they pertain to your business. Doctors are notorious for treating the illness, aliment, or disease rather than the patient. Too frequently we see in the newspaper that a doctor is being sued because he has performed a surgery on the wrong patient. Would this happen if the doctor spent 10 minutes with the patient learning who they are? This is a dramatic example; however, think about how little attention many businesses direct toward learning about their customers. This is not a discussion about making a single sale. The purpose of knowing our customers is to create lasting loyalty. When customers feel the only thing you know about them is the purchase they are considering, there is no sense of loyalty. They rightfully believe that you only recognize them or care about them as a sale. There is no relationship that encourages their return. When you do this, you are risking the economic equivalent of performing the wrong surgery.

Knowing and understanding your customer begins and ends with listening, speaking and learning. This isn't something you do once. Every time you are talking with your customers, you should use the opportunity to learn as much about them as possible.

After We Talk

This chapter is a discussion of how we can use effective communication to create loyalty. We have discussed effective communication as a means to establish a relationship *before* we do business with our customers and we have discussed the use of effective communication *while* we are doing business with our customers. Now let's look at the use of effective communication after we have conclude a business transaction.

How we communicate after we conclude a business transaction has the greatest impact on the relationship we have with our customers. Many businesses are focused solely on the immediate sale. Once a sale is concluded, these businesses don't do anything to maintain contact with their customers. Any effort you expend in maintaining contact will be noticed because most businesses don't make any attempt.

Newsletters, flyers, e-mail, and personalized letters are great ways to continue communicating with your customers. In general terms, the purpose of your continuing communication is to reinforce and repeat your value proposition, offer assurance, and most importantly, demonstrate your customer's importance.

Thank You Notes

Thanking your customers is the single most powerful way to communicate with them. A thank you note is tangible evidence of the customer's importance. The best way to thank them is with a handwritten note. A handwritten thank you note may seem very simple, but it is the most appreciated communication you can give. As simple as a thank you note is, it is also one of the least used methods of communicating to today's customers and clients. A thank you e-mail is better than nothing, but if you really want to get your customer's attention, send them a handwritten thank you note through the mail. The cost of the card and postage will be returned to you many times over in increased customer loyalty.

Moro Restaurant in Wilmington, Delaware, is an upscale eatery. The restaurant sends its customers thank you notes. Management says that handwritten notes go to all of their patrons who fill out a customer service card inserted with the check. These thank you notes emphasize the customers' importance and encourage them to come back.

Thank you notes should not be reserved just for thanking customers for buying something. You can send notes to thank customers f stopping in, listening to your sales story, referring others to you, and for purchases they might have made in the past. The critical factor in using thank you notes successfully is to be sincere. Sincerely thank your prospects and clients for their consideration, purchases, and whatever else is appropriate.

Traditionally, Realtors, car dealerships, insurance agents, and other professional salespeople send thank you notes after the customer makes a major purchase. Many of these businesses send their customers a tin of gourmet cookies or a complimentary dinner at a good restaurant. This is great, but it is also somewhat expected. If a thank you note is all the customer receives at the time of a major purchase, it will seem automated and sent out of obligation rather than as a sincere thank you.

Recently, I was doing some work with an insurance company in Indianapolis. I met a woman who is a vice president for the company, and she told me about her car-buying experiences. She drives a substantial distance every year and buys a new car every two years. She told me the only car she ever considers buying is a Mercury. She said, "When I bought my first Mercury, I got thank you notes from the sales department, service department, and the family who owns the dealership. I was impressed. But then I got a call from the factory. People who work in the Mercury factory regularly call customers to thank them and ask for advice in how to improve their cars. Nobody has ever called me from a car factory. They call about once or twice a year. They really appreciate my business. I wouldn't consider any other car."

Sincerely thanking your customers is the best way to demonstrate their importance. They will repay you with their loyalty.

Newsletters

During my career I have used newsletters to communicate with my customers on a regular basis. At times, I have used monthly and weekly newsletters. More recently I have been using a monthly e-mail newsletter, or e-zine.

My newsletters include current loyalty best practices, items from various business journals that pertain to customer relational management and customer loyalty management, and a personal observation tory.

As a writer and speaker on the subject of customer loyalty, my value proposition is quite clear. I help my clients develop activities that support the five principles that create customer loyalty. The purpose of my newsletter is to reinforce and repeat my value proposition. In addition, I use my newsletter to thank my readers.

The personal observation or story portion of my newsletter is the part that specifically reinforces one of the five principles. The following is a story I included in a recent newsletter. I hope you find this particular story interesting because first it demonstrates how casual an article can be, and second, it demonstrates how a major company is effectively communicating with their customers.

> Groucho Marx once said, "I wouldn't belong to a club that would have me as a member." I feel pretty much the same way. I don't count Sam's Discount Club or AAA as real clubs. I do belong to the Tennessee Squires. The Tennessee Squires is an organization that is run by the Jack Daniel's Distillery. There are no dues or membership costs. As a member, you are given 1 square inch of land in Lynchburg, Tennessee, the home of Jack Daniel's. Each piece of land is given a plot number. My land holdings in Tennessee can be summed up with the plot number f22455.
>
> The Jack Daniel's Distillery publishes a beautiful calendar every year and sends one to each Tennessee Squire. The calendar depicts scenery from around Lynchburg and Moore County, Tennessee. The best part of being a Tennessee Squire is the letters they send out three or four times a year. The following is a recent letter that came from the Lynchburg and Moore County Chamber of Commerce.
>
> Dear Mr. Lawfer
>
> A "weighty" issue has come up that you need to be aware of. It concerns our town dog. You see, Lynchburg has always had at least one town dog. Fritz, a very personable Irish Setter, held the honor for many years.
>
> After Fritz passed away, we went without a unique personality until the Cone Hound showed up. She earned her name by begging ice cream cones from tourists, and she's never been abo

snatching a cone from a hand held too low! The Cone Hound has become a fixture around here.

Well, the Cone Hound is getting quite plump, and now she's got the other dogs begging ice cream too. This was discussed at our last town meeting, and we agreed it's time to take action! It isn't their figures we're concerned about—it's their health. It will be hard to ignore those begging eyes, but for their own good we need to ask folks to stop feeding them ice cream. Help us keep our town dogs healthy.

Sincerely,

Larry Moorehead

One of the Squires' letters talked about an old tree that was near my property that had been struck by lightning. It seems there was a huge bee's nest in the tree and something had to be done. The letters are great fun. I really enjoy getting them.

Jack Daniel's Distillery makes bourbon. I'm not much of a bourbon drinker and my wife hardly ever drinks any spirits. A few weeks ago we were hosting a dinner party and I found myself at a liquor store stocking up on libations. I specifically needed bourbon, as we didn't have any for our guests.

The first thing I noticed was how much more Jack Daniel's cost than other bourbons. Old Gargle Puss cost about $15 for a bottle and Jack Daniel's cost about $23 for the same size bottle. I don't know that I was specifically thinking about the calendars and letters I had received from Jack Daniel's over the years, but I bought the bottle of Jack Daniel's bourbon. I'm not sure I can discern one bourbon from the other, but Jack Daniel's seemed to be the right brand to buy. After all, I am a Squire.

Now for an offer you may not be able to refuse: With the powers vested in me as a Tennessee Squire I can nominate other folks for Squirehood. If you'd like to become a Squire, send me an e-mail or give me a call.

After I sent this story with my newsletter, I got several calls and ails. Many of my readers enjoyed the story and wanted to be- a Squire. I completed the nomination forms for these readers and submitted them to Jack Daniel's. Since then, they have become Tennessee Squires, and have received the plot number for their 1 square inch of land, calendars, and the very entertaining letters to keep them informed of their land holdings in Tennessee. Every contact they receive from Jack Daniel's is a small reminder of me and how important they are to me.

I don't have any insider information about the general success or effectiveness of Jack Daniel's Tennessee Squire campaign, but I know it works on me and the many people I have told.

As a writer I have kept an inventory of stories that I can use in my newsletters. You can do the same by saving articles from newspapers and magazines that may be of interest to your customers. Use the information from the articles to make your own story. I am not suggesting that you plagiarize or violate copyright laws. For example, your industry's publications announce a new trend in the marketplace. You can use this information in your newsletter by offering how you think this trend will affect your customers or your local marketplace.

Your newsletter should be informative and if possible entertaining, but most importantly, it must be pertinent to your business and your customers. Your newsletter can include stories about how your product or service is being used. You can include success stories or testimonials from your customers (make sure to get their permission). Human interest or biographical stories about you or your staff can be very powerful in helping your customers recognize your efforts as people doing business with people.

My client Dr. Hall is a pathologist and president of a medium-sized pathology lab in the Northwest. There are eight pathologists in Dr. Hall's group. These physicians are totally dependent on other doctors in their community for work. Family practices, dermatologists, and other physicians in the community use Dr. Hall's group for lab testing. The practice is nearly 15 years old and uses only the most up-to-date equipment and practices. Because of its location and competition, this group offers the quickest turnaround time on all lab studies. But while the community it operates in has grown, this pathology practice has seen little or no increase in revenue over the last few years.

My initial study of this practice revealed total ignorance of the principle *people do business with people*. These doctors were providing a superior service but spent no time developing relationships with the referring physician who were providing them with all their work. The referring physicians sent tissue samples to the pathology group and got lab reports back. The referring physicians knew these pathologist only by their group name, Pathology Associates.

I recommended that each of the pathologists make routine phone calls to thank referring physicians for their business. We also developed a quarterly newsletter that features biographical and current information on the pathologists in the group. This information helps their customers identify these doctors on a personal and professional basis. Their newsletter includes information on new testing and lab equipment. This information reinforces the group's value proposition. As their customers got more familiar with these doctors and their value proposition, the group began to develop relationships that have led to a dramatic increase in their revenues. Central to this increase is the powerful use of their newsletter.

The point is that you can use a newsletter to demonstrate value by reinforcing and repeating your value proposition or by crafting your newsletter to address any of the other five principles that create loyalty.

There are several publishing services that offer industry-specific newsletters that can be personalized for your business. These boilerplate newsletters will keep your name in front of your customers, but they will do little to effectively communicate your value proposition or demonstrate your customer's importance. Your unique newsletter, even if it is not professionally produced, will be much more effective in telling your story. Your customers will detect your personal touch and will respond with interest and an understanding of their importance.

Thank you notes, birthday cards, and all other correspondence with your customers are more effective and therefore more valuable when they are personalized. Customers recognize your short hand-written note wishing them a happy birthday or congratulations as your personal sentiments, an expression of interest in them. Cards that have been preprinted or that offer a discount on the customer's birth-are only seen as advertisements or promotions.

Notifying your existing customers of a sale, special promotion, or the availability of a product before the public is notified is more effective than a notice or advertisement to the general public. Your customers have already demonstrated a willingness to do business with you. They will feel special and appreciated when they are the first to be notified. They are more likely to tell their friends about this insider information than they are to mention a general public announcement.

Be Careful of What You Say

Many businesses use notices and announcements to offer a special incentive to non-customers. This is the equivalent of telling your current customers that they are not as important as non-customers.

I use Comcast as my Internet service provider. The cable modem service costs about $50 per month. Every month or so I get a flyer in the mail from Comcast that announces a special offer of $19.95 per month for the first three months for new cable modem subscribers. These announcements encourage me to cancel my current subscription and start over as a new customer.

Several years ago, a major oil company offered a 5¢ per gallon discount to customers who paid in cash. This was during the period when it was popular for oil companies to issue their own credit cards. People who used the oil company's credit card were rewarded with the convenience of charging their gas purchases as an enticement for their loyalty. When the oil company offered cash-paying customers a discount, the customers using credit cards felt cheated. Many of these loyal customers chose to do business elsewhere—where they would be appreciated.

Most schemes that offer preferential treatment to new customers only attract customers who are willing to switch to any company that offers a lower price or a special promotion. Preferential treatment for loyal customers not only deepens loyalty, but also gives loyal customers something to talk about. Armed with better service, a better deal, recognition, or any clear value proposition, loyal customers are delighted to tell the world about your business. Every flyer, newslett or any other type of communication you send needs to tell the s of how and why your customers are special.

Comcast could entice new customers to their service by using testimonials from current customers. This would reinforce their value proposition to current subscribers while introducing new customers to the service. Every communication does not have to offer a special promotion. Keeping your customers and prospects aware of your unique value proposition is sufficient reason to send ongoing communications.

Automobile dealerships are notorious for continually promoting their businesses through special sales events. Their flyers and announcements usually mirror their radio and television advertisements. It seems every sale is the biggest sale they have ever had. They are always screaming that they are overstocked. The advertisement proclaims, "We are overstocked. We don't have space for all the new cars that are arriving daily!" Well, whose fault is that? They tell us, "We will sell all new cars for $1000 below invoice." What does that mean? Are they selling cars for $1000 less than what they paid for them? Don't these guys know how to run their business? "Drag it in. Push it in. We don't care what condition it's in. We'll give you $5000 for your old trade!" No wonder they're overstocked. Who's going to buy my old clunker for $5000? And on and on it goes.

The new car business is a multi-billion dollar industry. Despite my criticism, they sure do know how to sell cars. But do they know how to create loyalty? Do they effectively communicate to create loyalty?

Marketing and branding gurus rate the Saturn automobile as the second most valuable nameplate in the automotive industry. Saturn dealers don't have tent sales because they are overstocked. They don't lure customers with inflated claims. Instead, they invite their customers to picnics and homecomings at their Spring Hill, Tennessee, plant. Saturn sends a message of the "Saturn Family," a positive buying experience, and most importantly, a positive ownership experience. Saturn consistently sends a message of their unique value proposition and the importance of their customers. Loyalty is the reason the gurus rate Saturn the second most valuable brand. What message are you sending to your customers?

Rick is a Realtor in Daytona Beach, Florida. He specializes in ng and selling beachfront condominiums that are located in a block area. Rick sends his monthly newsletter to potential real estate customers and all the people that live in the one-block area where he sells real estate. Each newsletter has a list of all the properties that are for sale in that area. He is the listing agent on some of the properties while others are listed by other real estate agents. Each newsletter features a calendar of local events, a neighbor's favorite recipe, and a short biography of someone in the neighborhood. He does not offer any special enticements to list or buy property from him; however, he is the first person people call when they are considering a condominium in his territory. They know he cares about the neighborhood and is most familiar with the people and what is going on. His newsletter effectively communicates his value proposition, assurance, and the importance of his customers.

The point: Customers become loyal if you give them something to base their loyalty on. Your communications with your customers need to recognize their importance, thank them for their continuing loyalty, and reinforce your value proposition.

The frequency of newsletters, thank you notes, and other communications should be based on the amount of customer activity. A dry cleaner doesn't need to send a thank you note every time a customer drops off laundry. However, a calendar or semi-annual newsletter to customers would be quite appropriate. A Realtor, depending on sales activity, might consider a monthly or bi-monthly newsletter. Most retail stores can effectively communicate with their customers with a quarterly flyer or newsletter.

Remember the definition of a loyal customer? A loyal customer is a customer who does business with you on a repeat basis and is your advocate in their willingness to tell others about you. It's the second part of this definition: "...willing to tell others about you," that is also capitalized on through regular communications. A clever newsletter or incentive coupons delivered by your loyal customer to their friends and family is very powerful.

I distribute my current e-mail newsletter to 250 people. One of my clients resends my newsletter to more than 400 people on her distribution list. Another client resends the newsletter to more than 200 people. I am not sure what the total distribution is for my newsletter, but I know that I hear from new prospects every week that have been developed by my loyal customers.

Using effective communication to create loyalty is a continuum. We have discussed *before we talk* in terms of what we do to establish a relationship before we transact business. This is not something we do only once. It is important to establish or reestablish our relationship with our customers every time we meet with them. The object of our study is creating loyalty, which is repeat buying. Every meeting and every transaction are equally important, and are opportunities to further create and deepen loyalty. Establishing the relationship we have with our customers will affect every customer encounter and, therefore, every future encounter. Establishing a relationship *before we talk* reminds our customers of their importance. When we reestablish the relationship, we are telling our customer that today's meeting is a continuation of all our business dealings. We are telling our customer they are important because of the total relationship we have with them. Reestablishing the relationship *before we talk* defines and confirms even the smallest transaction as an integral part of the overall relationship you share.

Effective communication *when we talk* is a strategy for creating loyalty. I have described some specific techniques that you can use to lead your customers. More important than these techniques is the philosophy that offering leadership is a strategy. By knowing and understanding your customer, you are in a position to help them by means of your leadership. This leadership isn't something we do once and it's over. We should employ the strategy of leadership every time we talk with our customers. Continual leadership makes it clear that you are helping your customer. Without leadership, you are saying, "I don't know if this purchase is important to you, but it sure is important to me." Effectively communicating leadership when we talk creates loyalty.

Effectively communicating your value proposition, assurance, and the customer's importance after we talk is a process of encouraging your customer to buy from you again. This process, whether it is a regular newsletter, thank you note, or some other communication, invites and entices your customer to continue the relationship. When they accept your invitation and enticement, you are in a position to begin the sales cycle again by reestablishing the relationship before we talk.

Effectively communicating before we talk, when we talk, and after we talk perpetuates loyalty. Effective communication is a continuous process that brings your customers back to buy from you again and again and arms them with your message to share with everyone they know.

Summary

✓ Communication is the largest single factor determining what kinds of relationships we make with others and what happens to us in the world we live in.

✓ We communicate by what we say, how we say it, and how we look. This is how we judge people when we don't have any other information to base our judgment on.

✓ Effective communication is two-way. Effective communication is a combination of reactionary interpersonal skills. Speaking, listening, and learning are the basis for effective communication.

✓ The important points with regards to communicating with your customers:
   1. Establish a relationship at the beginning of every transaction.
   2. Remind customers on a regular basis of the importance of their loyalty through thank you notes.
   3. Lead customers in your discussions.
   4. Communicate with customers on a regular and frequent basis.

✓ The message you give to your internal and external customers and how you deliver that message is central to the process of creating loyalty.

Are you effectively communicating with your customers? Take this test and see.

Effective Communication Test

1. Do you establish or reestablish the relationship you have with your customers before every transaction? How do you do this?

2. Do you provide leadership when you are communicating with your customers? Give a few specific examples of how you provide this leadership.

3. Do your customers understand that you recognize their importance? How do you demonstrate their importance?

4. Do you regularly communicate with your customers? Give specific examples of how you regularly reinforce your value proposition and offer assurance to your customers.

5. Are you distributing regular newsletters, flyers, or other types of written communication?

6. Do your regular communications reinforce the principles of creating loyalty? Give specific examples of how each of the principles are utilized in your written communications.

7. Are your communications with customers based around making a sale or building a relationship? Give specific examples of relationship-building communications.

8. Have you armed your loyal customers with a simple message they can share with their family and friends regarding you and your business? What is this message?

9. Do your customers have tangible written evidence of your recognition of their importance? What is this evidence?

10. Communications are two-way. How do you listen to your customers? Do you listen before, during, and after each transaction? How do you use the information you have gained from listening to your customers? Give specific examples.

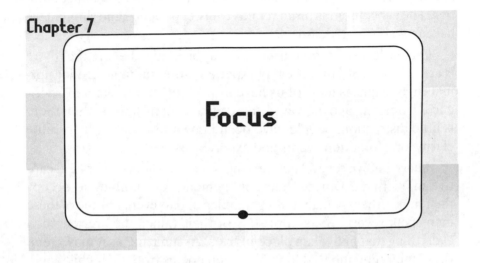

Chapter 7

Focus

Focus is the object of your current attention. All of your thoughts and actions are directed by your focus. If you are most interested in new customers, then that is where your attention will be focused. If you are most interested in creating loyalty, your attention must be focused on existing customers. The outcome of your effort is always a reflection of your focus. Focus affects customer loyalty in three ways:

1. How you think about yourself and your business.
2. How you think about your customers.
3. How your customers think about you.

First, let's examine how focus affects the way you think. The human brain and how we think can be separated into two categories: conscious and subconscious. The subconscious portion of the brain controls the automated functions of our bodies. It governs body temperature, controls digestion, dilates and contracts the pupils of the eye, regulates heart rate, adjusts metabolism, and manages all functions of our physical being. This part of the brain also records our memories. The subconscious brain retains every experience and thought we have from birth till death.

On one level of consciousness, it may be hard to believe that there is actually a record of our every experience and thought. Under normal circumstances most of us have little ability to remember experiences from long ago; however, in extreme circumstances when there is little distraction, people have been known to recall with absolute clarity long forgotten events and experiences.

I have known several people who were prisoners of war held captive in Vietnam. During their confinement, with nothing to occupy their minds, they spent their time thinking of past events. Some of these men spent several years in prison. In their minds they reexamined everything that had taken place in lives. As amazing as it may seem, these men remembered long-forgotten poems from their childhood. Poems that they had not thought of in many years returned to their consciousness. They learned they could recite these poems line for line. Bible passages and foreign language words and phrases emerged after deep thought. Everything they had ever learned was still available to them, only it was buried deep in their subconscious minds.

Of equal importance in understanding the subconscious mind is the recognition that this part of our brain is not rational. The subconscious mind records everything without judging the information. It is as if our subconscious mind is a tape recorder. It records information without validating importance or truthfulness. As soon as our subconscious mind accepts an idea, it proceeds to put it into effect immediately. It works by association of ideas and uses every bit of knowledge that we have gathered in our lifetime to bring about its purpose.

For example, you are getting ready to walk out the door. You usually leave your keys on the table by the door, but you look at the table and your keys are gone. You announce, "I can't find my keys." Your subconscious mind takes this information and immediately uses its full power to prevent you from finding your keys. As long as you repeat the phrase, "I can't find my keys," you won't find them.

If instead you would have said, "I don't see my keys, but I'll find them in a minute." Your subconscious mind would recognize this command and immediately use its full power to locate your keys.

The subconscious mind is somewhat like a vending machine. If you deposit the right amount of money, the vending machine gives you a candy bar. The vending machine isn't rational; it only does what it is told to do. You could cram a $100 bill into the vending machine and it wouldn't give you anything. Give it 50¢ and it gives you the candy bar. The subconscious mind, like the vending machine, is irrational. The subconscious mind cannot compare information and make decisions.

The conscious mind is rational; it compares information and makes decisions. It is forever making comparisons and judging and assessing the validity of every thought and experience. The conscious mind can only deal with one thought at a time; however, these single thoughts are being processed at lightning speed.

We can compare the conscious and subconscious minds by thinking of a large ship. On the bridge of the ship is the captain; the captain is our conscious mind. His job is to make sure that the ship reaches its destination. The captain is considering the speed of the ship, the wind, ocean currents, and the ship's proximity to land. He compares all this information before he gives a command to the men working below deck in the engine room. The men in the engine room represent our subconscious mind. Their job is to follow orders. They don't know where the ship is going; they only follow orders. If the captain says full speed ahead, the engine room opens the throttle wide. They don't know if the ship is close to rocks or shallow water, or even what direction the ship is traveling, they only follow the orders of the captain.

Here's the part that is most useful: While the subconscious mind is doing an infinite amount of things simultaneously, the conscious mind only deals with one thought at a time. You determine each of the thoughts being processed by your conscious mind.

Let's examine one more element of how we think before we apply this information to our quest for loyal customers. The reticular activating system controls which part of the mind will deal with a given issue. For example, in the morning you put on a wristwatch. While you are attaching the watch, your conscious mind is in control of your thoughts. This part of your brain is monitoring the procedure to make sure the watch is fastened properly and won't fall off. It told you which arm to put the watch on, detects the tightness of the band, and everything else associated with this task.

Once you have attached your watch, the reticular activating system moves all thoughts about your watch to your subconscious mind. If you had to always think about your watch, you would not be able to do anything else. You couldn't work, read a book, or have a conversation because you would be totally occupied with your watch. But the reticular activating system will notify you if the anything unusual happens. If the band breaks or the strap comes undone, the reticular activating system immediately sends a message to your conscious mind notifying you to redirect your attention away from whatever you're doing and take care of the watch.

You can see the reticular activating system at work when you buy a new car. For example, you buy a blue Buick thinking it will be the only one in your neighborhood. On the way home from the dealership, every other car you see is a blue Buick. The reticular activating system has noticed the importance of your decision and is on guard for all blue Buicks. Because the reticular activating system is working at all times, you are free to use your conscious mind for whatever purpose you choose. You do not choose the activities of your subconscious mind, but you are in total command of your conscious mind. You choose what you think about and what you focus on.

This ability to focus is the determining factor of everything that happens in your life. Albert Einstein stated the whole matter succinctly when he said, "The world we see is the world we are." The psychologist Denis Waitley said, "The world we see is the only world we know." In other words, our inner world represents our habitual thinking, beliefs, opinions, imagery, training, and indoctrination. We are perpetually projecting this inner state of mind onto people, conditions, and events. We look at people and conditions through the content of mental imagery. Everything we see and experience is filtered and bent through the prism of our minds. You might say that the whole world turns between your ears. If we see the world as hostile, we will live in a hostile world. If we see the world as wondrous, we will be filled with wonder and curiosity.

It is the thoughts that habitually occupy our minds that determine our world. Our deepest thoughts determine the world we see because what we think about becomes objectified in our lives. What we think about is what we see. We control what we think about and, therefore, control what we see. Ultimately, what we see becomes our reality. Our deepest thoughts are objectified in our lives.

This Pilot Benefits From His Deepest Thoughts

My father, Larry Lawfer, is 80 years old. Shortly after World War II, my father was working as a pilot for the Air National Guard in Bangor, Maine. His pay was based on his flight hours, so he volunteered for every flight that was available. This put him in a situation of flying with other pilots he may or may not have flown with before.

On January 11, 1949, my father volunteered to serve as copilot with a pilot he had never met. My father was eager to make the flight and didn't give much thought to the qualifications of the pilot who would be the captain on the flight. His eagerness for earning flight pay overruled what should have been his better judgment.

My father's first suspicions that something was wrong came as the captain began his approach to the runway. The captain was making the approach with the wind at their tail. The plane touched down on its main wheels but the tail wind continued pushing them down the runway. My father yelled, "Full throttle. Go 'round!" but the captain was convinced they could bring the plane to a stop before they ran out of runway. Unable to slow down, the plane crashed through a fence and into a thicket of trees. My father's back, both arms, and his right leg were broken.

My father wore casts on his arms and leg for four months, but he had to wear a body cast that immobilized his back for more than a year.

During his recuperation, my father learned that he could use a coat hanger to scratch frequent itching under the cast. During the day coat hangers protruded from every opening on his cast. He looked like a small radio station with antennas shooting out everywhere.

Every night he lulled himself to sleep chanting, "When I get this cast off I'll never have a back problem again." He repeated this chant every morning when he awoke. His subconscious mind accepted his chant as a command. This part of his brain accepted the idea as truth and proceeded to put it into effect immediately. It used the association of ideas and every bit of knowledge that he had gathered in his lifetime to bring about this purpose.

In 1950, my father's body cast was removed. His doctors told him his back was healed but he should expect backaches and pains for the rest of his life. During the more than 50 intervening years since the accident my father has never had a backache of any sort. He enjoys perfect health. His subconscious mind is perpetually at work serving the purpose of his command.

My father experiences the power of his subconscious mind every day. His experience is internal in nature; he affected his own body. This same power is available to affect the world around us.

This Ballplayer Learned How to Focus

Do you know of Frank Bettger? He was a professional baseball player in the early 1900s, who played for Johnstown, Pennsylvania, in the Tri-State League. He was young, ambitious, and wanted to get to the top—then he was fired. The coach, Bert Conn, told Frank, "You're lazy. You drag yourself around the field like a veteran who has been playing ball for 20 years. Why do you act that way if you're not lazy?"

Frank told his coach, "I'm so nervous, so scared, that I want to hide my fear from the crowd, especially from the other players on the team. I hope that by taking it easy I'll get rid of my nervousness."

Frank's coach said, "Frank, it will never work. That's the thing that is holding you down. Whatever you do after you leave here, for heaven's sake, wake yourself up, and put some life and enthusiasm into your work."

Frank had been making $175 a month at Johnstown. Remember, this was in the early 1900s, so $175 a month was pretty impressive. After being fired, Frank went to Chester, Pennsylvania, to work in the Atlantic League. His pay was $25 per month. Frank didn't think he could be very enthusiastic making $25 a month, but eventually, he did begin to act enthusiastic. After being on the Chester team for three days, an old ball player, Danny Meehan, came up to Frank and said, "Frank what in the world are you doing here in a rank bush-league?" Frank told him, "Well, Danny, if I knew how to get a better job, I'd go anywhere."

A week later, Danny encouraged the New Haven, Connecticut, team to give Frank a trial. No one knew Frank in that league, so he made a resolution that nobody would ever accuse Frank Bettger of being lazy. He made up his mind to establish a reputation of being the most enthusiastic ball player they'd ever seen. He thought that if he could establish such a reputation then he would have to live up to it.

From the moment he arrived on the field he acted like a man electrified; he acted as though he was alive with a million batteries. He threw the ball around the diamond so fast and hard that he almost knocked the other players down. Once, apparently trapped, Frank slid into third base with such force that the third baseman fumbled the ball and Frank was able to score an important run. The thermometer that day was showing 100 degrees, so no one would have been surprised if Frank dropped over with sunstroke the way he was running around the field.

Did it work? It worked like magic. Three things happened:

1. His enthusiasm almost entirely overcame his fear.
2. His enthusiasm affected the other players on the team. They, too, became enthusiastic.
3. Instead of dropping from the heat, he felt better during and after the game. He felt better than he had ever felt before.

Frank's biggest thrill came the next day when he read the New Haven newspaper: "This new player, Bettger, has a barrel of enthusiasm. He inspired our boys. They not only won the game, but also looked better than they have all season." The newspaper began calling him "Pep" Bettger.

Within 10 days Frank's income went from $25 a month to $185 a month—a 700-percent increase. He got the stupendous increase in income not because he could throw a ball better, catch better, or hit better, not because he had any more ability as a ball player.

Within two years of the time Frank was hoping to get the $25 a month job with the Chester team, he was playing for the St. Louis Cardinals and making 30 times as much as he had made in the minor league.

What happened? Frank discovered one of the great secrets of life. He acted a certain way and then began to feel that way. Soon after, he *was* that way. Frank didn't have anything to be enthusiastic about, but he acted enthusiastic. After acting enthusiastically, he began to feel enthusiastic. And from his feelings of enthusiasm he became enthusiastic. He learned the lesson of focus. What you focus on will become your reality.

Frank Bettger became a part of the Dale Carnegie organization and repeated this story hundreds times to audiences all over the world and included it in his book, *How I Raised Myself from Failure to Success in Selling*.

The story of my father's accident and how he dealt with it illustrates the ability to affect our world internally. When my father consciously told himself he would never again experience a backache, he was commanding his subconscious to make it true. This entire process and outcome was internal to my father. On the other hand, Frank Bettger's story illustrates how this same process can change the world around us. Frank consciously thought about acting enthusiastic. His subconscious mind took this command and made Frank feel enthusiastic. Acting and feeling enthusiastic led to being enthusiastic. This enthusiasm influenced the people surrounding Frank. Frank's thoughts objectified themselves in his external world. Our conscious thoughts affect our subconscious minds and become reality in the world we live. What we think about manifests in our lives both internally and externally.

This phenomenon is known as the law of life. The law of life is also known as the law of belief. Simply stated, the law of belief says, "We don't always get what we want, but we do always get what we truly believe." What we truly believe becomes a self-fulfilling prophecy. This prophecy begins with our deepest habitual thoughts. These thoughts are accepted by the subconscious mind and are recorded as our reality. This reality objectifies itself in our world and completes the prophecy. The three phases are belief, results, and recognition. Because we believe, we get results. Because we see results, we recognize our beliefs and the process begins again.

So what do broken bones, baseball, and how our brains work have to do with getting your customers to buy from you again and again? Your deepest thoughts and what you focus on as a businessperson or sales professional will determine your reality. If you are focusing on getting new customers, you will, in fact, do the things necessary to gain new customers. If you are focusing on customer loyalty, your thoughts will drive you to serve your existing customers. This is the first of three ways focus affects customer loyalty. Focus determines how we think about our business and ourselves.

How We Think About Our Customers

The second way focus affects loyalty is by how we think about our customers. You determine the thoughts of your conscious mind and, therefore, determine your focus. This process is not limited to any one part of your life; it affects every aspect of your life. In your business life, you are influenced by external factors. The rewards, recognition, and compensation you receive are external factors and influence your thoughts. If you receive more rewards, recognition, or compensation from dealing with new customers, then your thoughts will be focused on this activity. If you receive more rewards, recognition, or compensation from dealing with existing customers, then your thoughts will be focused on activities that serve this group.

My esteemed reader, you are holding a copy of *Why Customers Come Back* in your hands at this moment. Previous pages of this book have described the principles of:

✓ People do business with people.

✓ Differentiation.

✓ Value and assurance.

✓ Effective communication.

When you make these principles a part of your deepest thoughts, you are instructing your subconscious mind to use its infinite power to serve your purpose. When you focus on the principles that create loyalty, you are instructing your subconscious mind to use your collective information to think about customers as being loyal.

Choices

Everything in life is about choices. Everything that has happened to you or will ever happen to you is a function of the choices you have already made or will make. When you focus on loyal customers, you are making a choice that will have a great impact on how you do business. You will move from forever searching for new customers to forever improving how you deal with current, loyal, repeat customers.

There is a wonderful experiment that helps explain the benefits of focus. The experiment is known as the Funnel Experiment and was developed by W. Edwards Deming, the father of modern management, to describe variations in manufacturing processes.

In the experiment, a funnel is mounted on a fixture with the small opening of the funnel pointed downward. The small opening of the funnel is suspended about 1 1/2 feet above a large paper target that measures 3 x 3 feet. A marble that is slightly smaller than the small opening on the funnel is dropped into the funnel. The marble falls through the hole and comes to rest on the paper. A small mark is made to note where the marble lands.

In the experiment, this process is repeated a few hundred times. A circle is drawn around all the marks that note where the marble has landed. The circle is no bigger than an inch or two in diameter. All of the marks could be covered with a teacup. There is little human intervention in this part of the experiment, so the marble lands in slightly different spots because of random chance. The size of the circle represents this natural variation. This natural variation is passive because there are no changes to the system.

In the second part of the experiment, the marble is dropped through the funnel and its landing spot is marked. This spot is the bull's-eye. A second marble is dropped through the funnel and its landing spot is marked. The difference between the bull's-eye and the landing spot for the second marble is precisely measured. The funnel is adjusted according to this difference. If, for example, the second marble lands 1/2 inch to the right of the bull's-eye, the funnel is moved 1/2 inch to the left to adjust the aim. A third marble is dropped and, once again, the funnel is adjusted to correct the aim. This process is repeated a few hundred times. A circle is drawn around all the landing spots. This time the circle is nearly as big as the entire 3 x 3 feet piece of paper. This circle represents active, or controlled, variation.

The results from this experiment show that passive, or random, variation produces a small circle. Active, or controlled, variation produces a much larger circle.

In manufacturing, the lesson of this experiment has to do with management and human intervention. When equipment and processes are allowed to operate without adjustment, quality is a known factor and predictable within close margins. When equipment and processes are forever being adjusted or changed, quality and predictability decrease dramatically. Deming advised manufacturers to recognize this phenomenon and operate systems on a passive basis. Change or adjustment should be in the form of refinements to the system, not the operation of the system or the system itself.

For example, in the experiment, Deming's theory would suggest a funnel with a smaller opening or a more perfectly round marble. Deming would say make improvements to the materials, but do not change the system.

Let's apply this information to the principles that create loyalty: Joe owns All County Appliance Repair. Joe has a fleet of trucks and a staff of repair technicians that are on call to repair washing machines, refrigerators, stoves, and other household appliances. All County's value proposition is "same day service." All County is well known as a reputable business providing a dependable service. Any improvement Joe makes to the business should focus on his current value proposition. If Joe expands his inventory to include parts and supplies for a greater variety of brands, he is refining his value proposition. Longer hours and emergency service on the weekend further enhances his value proposition. His clearly defined value proposition increases customer loyalty because customers know what they can expect from All County. These refinements are equivalent to narrowing the hole on the funnel or using a more perfectly round marble in the experiment.

Joe's business is doing so well that he decides to expand. He decides to offer new appliances as well as the repair services. From the customer's perspective, this is really a new business endeavor. Some of his customers might buy a new refrigerator from him, but more likely they will be confused. They'll wonder if Joe is really more interested in selling appliances than offering repair services. They'll be suspicious about repair estimates. "Is Joe telling me the truth about the condition of my refrigerator? Is he raising the price on the repair to influence me to buy a new appliance?" Selling new appliances does not enhance Joe's value proposition for his repair business. Selling new appliances is the equivalent of adjusting the funnel in our experimen It is changing the system or introducing a new system rather th refining or improving the current system. The results become less predictable. His value proposition is not focused, and the task of creating loyal customers has become more difficult.

I'm not suggesting that Joe shouldn't sell new appliances; he can open a new business across town that sells new appliances. This new business can have its own value proposition. The new business can have a value proposition, assurance, and differentiators that focus on customers of the new enterprise. Joe's new endeavor should represent another system.

The point is that a value proposition has to be focused to be effective. A differentiator must be focused to be effective. A single business that does dry cleaning, sells casualty insurance, and offers fresh produce has little chance of developing a loyal clientele.

Many major American businesses totally ignore the principle of focus. Mergers and acquisitions, product line extensions, and new product lines are seldom entered into with the goal of benefiting customers. More likely these tactics are used to exploit customers.

Mutual Benefit is an insurance company with a 150-year history. The company had a loyal clientele demonstrated by its high retention of policyholders. Mutual Benefit believed it could sell investments and investment advice to these same policyholders. The company reasoned that its clients were already familiar with and trusted the company. Mutual Benefit was motivated more by additional revenue than service to its clients. The company was not focusing on improving or refining their insurance products, it was introducing an entirely different product line. In relation to the Funnel Experiment, they were moving the funnel wildly rather than improving the marble. Ultimately, Mutual Benefit became one of the largest insurers to ever file reorganizational bankruptcy.

But Mutual Benefit was not alone. Many major companies bought other unrelated or barely related businesses in hopes of exploiting their relationships with customers. Gartner, the IT research firm, purchased Tech Republic, the online information service, for $80 million. Within two years, it sold Tech Republic for less than $30 million. This was an expensive lesson by anyone's standard. Xerox went into the financial service marketplace and learned the same lesson. Kodak's venture into pharmaceuticals was a similar lesson. Coca-Cola and

Transamerica learned the same lesson from their experiences in the movie business. Ford Motor Company, General Electric, and a host of other companies have spent enormous sums to purchase companies only to have to divest themselves of their acquisitions for pennies on the dollar. The activities of these companies demonstrate their lack of focus on their existing customers.

The process of becoming more focused can be intimidating. You may feel that narrowing your value proposition will limit your customer base. You may be skeptical of focusing and just depending on current customers instead of developing new customers. Your skepticism can be reversed: Focus your thoughts and use the powers of your subconscious mind.

What Is Success?

What is your definition of success? Many people feel that reaching a goal is success. A salesperson might believe that making the sale is success. I think the best definition of success is: "Making progress towards a worthwhile goal."

Think about raising children. Think about success in raising children. When do you become successful in raising your children? Is success attained when your children graduate from college, get married, have children of their own, or retire successfully? At what point do you proclaim success for raising your children?

Raising children to be good citizens; productive workers; and happy, fulfilled individuals is a worthwhile goal. I also think the process of raising children continues throughout the parents' and the child's life. However, I believe success can be proclaimed all along the way. You are successful when you are making progress towards a worthwhile goal. When you are able to teach little Johnny the benefits of bathroom etiquette, you are successful. When little Alice learns to get along with other classmates, you are successful. All along the path of raising children you can be successful. You do not have to wait until little Sally becomes CEO of Acme Worldwide Services to proclaim yourself, or little Sally, successful. Success is making progress along the way toward a worthwhile goal. At any point in the child-rearing process you may be skeptical of the overall outcome

You may have doubts and wonder if your child will be the only kid attending college with a pacifier and dragging a teddy bear around. Relax. The key to current success is commitment. Once you commit to the accomplishment of a worthwhile goal, you've made the step. You are successful as soon as you begin to see progress.

Developing customer loyalty is a worthwhile goal. Your life and your customers' lives will be enhanced through a relationship of loyalty. Your life is enhanced because you are rewarded financially in ever-greater proportions, and you have brought greater value to others. Your customers' lives have been enhanced because they have a de-pendable supplier that understands them and delivers goods and ser-vices in a way that earns their loyalty. When you proclaim customer loyalty as your goal, you are committing your conscious and subcon-scious mental resources to this accomplishment. Your success begins with the proclamation.

Do you know about O. Alfred Granum and the One Card System? Granum developed a selling method he called the One Card System, which is used by insurance agents and other sales professionals all over the world. The One Card System uses 3 x 5 index cards to store information about a prospect. The salesperson writes down as much information as is known about a prospect on the card and files the card by the next contact date. Over a period of time, the salesperson develops information about the prospect and continues to contact the prospect on a periodic basis. For the most part, the salesperson places more value on the prospect's name and other information they have gathered than on making a sale. The idea is that with enough contact over a period of time, the prospect will do business with you. Probably most important is the salesperson's feeling of inevita-bility that the prospect will eventually do business with him or her.

Granum's method is really based on the notion of building a rela-tionship to produce loyalty. If the salesperson treats the prospect in a loyal manner, eventually most prospects will treat the salesperson with responding loyalty. It begins with the salesperson's belief and mani-fests in the customer's eventual purchase. Salespeople who use this method send birthday and holiday cards, notes of congratulations when the prospect gets recognition in the newspaper, and they follow up on a periodic basis through phone contact. The salesperson treats the prospect as a loyal customer. The Granum method is really terrific because it causes the salesperson to focus on customer relationships rather than on a sale.

Many salespeople want to first identify their most loyal clients and then treat them as loyal clients. Granum teaches us to first identify a group of prospects as the people we would like to be loyal customers. Then we begin treating them as if they were already loyal. Granum's message is that before you see and receive, you have to believe and give.

The ability to focus on the relationship rather than on making a sale is critical in developing customer loyalty. We want our clients and customers to be loyal. If we want our customers to buy from us on a repeat basis and to freely encourage others to buy from us, we must take the first step and believe in them and treat them as loyal customers. Our focus must be: *The customer I am dealing with right now deserves everything I have to give to my most loyal customer.* Every prospect I have has the capacity to be my most loyal customer. By maintaining this focus, we are encouraging and creating loyalty.

A Business Based on Belief in Loyal Customers

William W. Grainger founded his company in Chicago in 1927. He wanted to provide an efficient solution for customers who wanted to access a consistent supply of electric motors. At that time, Grainger published what he called *The MotorBook*. *The MotorBook* was more than just a sales catalog for electric motors, it was a complete resource for anyone wanting to learn about electric motors—how they worked, comparisons, applications, and specifications. *The MotorBook* was free to customers, prospects, and even competitors; Grainger was willing to freely share the information he had gathered. Grainger believed that anyone who had an interest in electric motors would eventually become a loyal customer. His competitors would not think of sharing their intellectual capital, while Grainger gave it away in his *MotorBook*.

Today, W.W. Grainger is a Fortune 500 company and has more than 600 locations throughout North America. Grainger is focused on helping its customers complete their jobs successfully by providing them with the right product at the right time with the right information.

The MotorBook is now known as the W.W. Grainger Catalog. Contractors, facility operators, and many others depend on the Grainger Catalog as the most accurate source of information for the materials and supplies that they buy.

The W.W. Grainger Catalog contains information on electric motors, casters, compressors, industrial supplies, and lighting fixtures, material handling, safety and emergency preparedness equipment, and several other product categories. The catalog offers more than just information on the brands that Grainger sells. The catalog provides detailed specifications and product applications for all brands.

Many companies provide detailed information on their own products in their catalogs or on their Websites, but Grainger's information goes much further: It provides a detailed guide of industry standards. Grainger's catalog is a valuable resource whether or not you buy anything from Grainger. The Grainger philosophy of keeping customers well informed and well equipped extends beyond just Grainger's customers: Grainger is freely providing information to everyone.

Grainger's philosophy focuses on providing value. Its philosophy demonstrates focus on loyal customers. Grainger believes that anyone with an interest in electric motor and industrial supplies will eventually become a loyal customer. It is not waiting for the prospect to buy something; it provides value before the sale. Grainger believes in and sees loyal customers because of its focus on loyalty. Grainger has grown into a multi-billion dollar company by focusing on customer loyalty. It is constantly getting new customers by focusing on its existing customers.

Contrast W.W. Grainger to a company that is focused on getting new customers. This other company tells its prospects that once you become a paying customer, you will have access to all the company's resources. This company is not focused on customer loyalty; instead, it is using the benefits of being a customer to attract new buyers. Its focus is really on getting new customers.

The year 2001 proved challenging for W.W. Grainger. As the economic climate in North America turned progressively weaker, its sales declined 4.5 percent. Despite this decline in revenue, Grainger had an increase in profitability. It enjoys the benefits of customer loyalty cause it focuses on loyal customers.

We have discussed how we think about our businesses and our-selves, and how we think about our customers. We have also dis-cussed how our minds work relative to objectifying our deepest thoughts. Equally important is how our customers think about us.

How Our Customers Think About Us

Loyalty is the cumulative result and response to specific interper-sonal activities. Immediate benefits can be demonstrated from the application of any of these specific activities, but the best results come from your customers' long-term continuing relationship with you. This relationship is based in part on your customers' belief of their impor-tance to you. When your activities move from your loyal customers to acquiring new customers, your focus has shifted. Your loyal custom-ers are no longer your most important asset. Your focus is on new customers. Everything you do to acquire new customers will be sus-pect by your current loyal customers.

Every business wants new customers because new customers are how a business grows. However, the best path to acquiring new cus-tomers is through your focus on current customers.

When businesses offer first-time buyer incentives or special deals for new customers, they are defining their priority. Their number one priority is getting new customers. They are focused on new custom-ers. Prospects are more important than loyal customers and loyal cus-tomers are aware of the business's focus.

I mentioned in an earlier chapter that Comcast is my Internet service provider. I have subscribed to Comcast's service for a couple of years. I pay Comcast about $50 a month for the high-speed cable service. Comcast solicits new customers by offering the same service I subscribe to for only $19.95 a month for the first three months. Comcast is more focused on new customers than they are on me, a long-time customer. I am still using the service, but if a competitor comes to town, I don't feel any commitment to staying with Comcast. Why should I? Comcast isn't committed to me.

Banks are notorious for offering new customers a better deal than they offer their existing customers. Many banks offer stadium blankets, digital cameras, or other incentives to new customers. In some cases they offer free banking services, such as traveler's checks, to new customers while they charge their existing customers for this same service. Recognizing this preferential treatment for new customers, many people are forever changing where they do their banking.

Several businesses have used special offers to attract first-time customers. These schemes invariably send a message to loyal customers that new customers are more important. In addition, new customers who are attracted by the special offer are less likely to return after they have received the one-time benefit.

Businesses that want to create customer loyalty must focus on loyal customers. Focus is the object of your current attention. The conscious mind can only process one thought at a time. You can't be focused on loyal customers if you are spending your time and resources on trying to attract new customers. Your focus determines how you think and how your customers think of you.

Getting New Customers by Focusing on Current Customers

World Class Catamarans is a privately owned company in Tarboro, North Carolina. The company is relatively small in comparison to the marine industry in general. World Class Catamarans builds boats by the hundreds while marine giants such as Genmar build boats by the thousands.

World Class Catamarans prides itself on building great boats that exceed its customers' expectations. It claims that building a long-term family relationship with its customers is its ambition, and creating and nurturing an organization that will prosper and grow for the benefit of its customers and employees is its vision.

The only way World Class Catamaran makes any money is by selling new boats. New customers are their only source of revenue. Boat owners are not like car buyers who trade their old car in for a new model every couple of years. Unless a boat owner is trading for a larger or smaller boat, they typically keep their boats for several years. Even still, World Class isn't focused on new customers; it is focused on its existing customers.

World Class Catamarans sponsors Owner Rendezvous, where its customers can meet and vacation together. Customers of World Class are notified and invited to boat shows and other events whenever they are held near the customer's home. World Class Catamarans uses every opportunity to invite customers to stay in touch with their local dealers and the company. The company is truly living up to their claimed desire of building a long-term family relationship with its customers.

Mike O'Connell, World Class Catamaran's CEO, is committed to his customers. Rather than spending $10,000 on an advertisement in a boating magazine, Mike offered World Class boat owners a free polo shirt and ball cap displaying the company's logo. I recently visited with Mike and he told me, "Our loyal customers are our best advertising. We want to grow the company through our customers." The company is seeing substantial growth coming from its customers who introduce their friends and families to its unique line of boats and way of doing business.

Focusing on New Customers and Losing Loyal Customers

Belknap Hardware first set up shop on the banks of the Ohio River in Louisville, Kentucky, in 1840. The company started humbly in a small shop that produced iron products such as horse and mule shoes, nails, spikes, and other forged items.

When Belknap Hardware celebrated its 100th anniversary in 1940, it had grown to a complex of 37 buildings, including a network of connecting underground passageways and covered bridges throughout the property. Belknap Hardware was among the nation's largest wholesale enterprises with nationally recognized quality brands. The company was built on providing quality, affordable tools, with brand names such as Belknap, King of the Bluegrass and Thoroughbred, reflecting Kentucky's pride in its unique topography and its love of fine thoroughbred horses.

The company philosophy was that whether customers needed builder's hardware, housewares, mechanics' tools, farming tools, or even pocketknives, Belknap would fill that order with quality merchandise.

In 1880, Belknap's inventory was a mere 100 items. By 1940, the company's catalog had grown into a 3000-page tome, containing more than 75,000 items. In 1985, Belknap's inventory had reached more than 117,000 items.

Belknap, similar to other major hardware houses, faced many challenges and underwent many changes over the course of more than a century of operation. However, the company retained a "family" approach with its employees and their dependents, providing picnics, parties, and offering promotions from within the company rather than recruiting from outside. Belknap was a career for most of its employees.

The business changed over the years and was no longer just a retailer of hardware and supplies, but instead had become a wholesaler and distributor to other retail hardware stores throughout the country. The company grew and thrived on providing its loyal customers with household hardware, repair parts, tools, fasteners, and the thousands of other items shoppers expect to find in their neighborhood hardware store. Belknap differentiated itself by its huge inventory of thousands of items.

Belknap was sold to an investor in the mid-1980s. New ownership brought new management and new ideas. Almost immediately after taking charge of the historic hardware company, new management declared the huge number of items in Belknap's inventory to be a waste. Employees who had spent their entire careers at Belknap knew the company's strength came from its loyal customers who depended on the company's broad and deep inventory. Rather than serving its loyal clientele, management forged a new path for Belknap. The new Belknap scrapped thousands of items from its inventory and issued a new streamlined catalog. Within a few months Belknap had lost most of its loyal customers and was forced into bankruptcy. The company closed its doors forever in 1986. Belknap lost its loyal customer base becaused it failed to stay focused on the people who had made the company successful for so many years.

A final thought about focus: The businesses you compete against should not enter your thinking as you focus on creating loyalty. Focusing your attention on the competition diverts you from accomplishment.

Professional golfers provide insight into this phenomenon. Golfers play with other golfers, but they do not necessarily play against other golfers on the professional tour. For example, it's a sudden-death play-off and only Tiger Woods and Phil Mickelson are left in the tournament. Tiger isn't thinking about Phil. Tiger's total focus is on his own game—and only that. This focus allows Tiger to play his best.

You dilute and divert your energy when you focus on the competition. Remember, you control your focus and your focus determines your success.

Summary

✓ Focus affects loyalty in three ways: How you think about yourself and your business, how you think about your customers, and how your customers think about you.

✓ Your subconscious mind is irrational and records everything without judging the information. It works by association of ideas and uses every bit of knowledge that we have gathered in our lifetime to bring about its purpose.

✓ The conscious mind is rational; it compares information and makes decisions. The conscious mind can only deal with one thought at a time; however, these single thoughts are being processed at the speed of light.

✓ Our thoughts become objectified in our lives. What we think about is what we see. Ultimately, what we see becomes our reality. What we truly believe becomes a self-fulfilling prophecy.

✓ When you make the principles that create loyalty a part of your deepest thoughts, you are instructing your subconscious mind to use its infinite powers to serve your purpose.

✓ Developing your ability to focus on relationships instead of just making a sale is critical in creating customer loyalty.

In this chapter we discussed focus. Focus is all about turning your efforts toward building relationships rather than hunting for a sale. Take this test to see how well you use this principle.

Where Is Your Focus?

1. Do you spend more time and money prospecting for new customers or focusing on your current customers? Can you quantify your efforts?

2. Do you offer new customers special pricing or terms that are not available to loyal customers?

3. Do you have a clear vision of who your loyal internal and external customers are? Do you reward or recognize these customers? How do you reward and recognize these customers?

4. Would you cancel or delay a meeting with a current customer in order to meet with a prospect? Why?

5. Are you compensated and rewarded more for dealing with new customers or current customers?

6. Do you have a clear vision of your future and the future of your business? What is this vision?

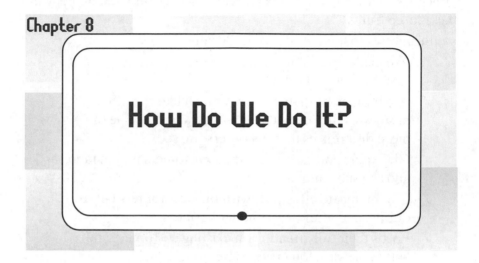

Chapter 8

How Do We Do It?

There are three truths that surround customer loyalty:

1. All profit comes from loyal customers. The cost of attracting and learning how to deal with a new customer is more than the profit you can earn on the first sale.

2. Customer loyalty is only an activity. All the goodwill and high emotions customers may have toward you is worthless unless they either buy from you or refer customers to you on a regular basis.

3. Customer satisfaction and customer loyalty are two different things. Customers may be satisfied with your products or services, but that doesn't mean they will repeatedly buy from you or refer people to you.

Your understanding of these three truths is important. If you do not agree with these three truths, you should reread the earlier chapters until you have an understanding. Learning how to apply the principles of loyalty will be meaningless to you until you agree with these three truths.

Businesses that create customer loyalty:

- ✓ Are made up of individual people recognizing customers as individual people.
- ✓ Are businesses that are pretty much like the other businesses they compete against, except for one or more differences that customers can see.
- ✓ Give value and assurances their customers understand and can substantiate.
- ✓ Communicate effectively with their customers before, during, and after they conduct business.
- ✓ Focus their full attention on existing customers and getting new customers to come back.

The principles that create loyalty are intuitive, but developing the specific activities that support them is critical. Practice doesn't make perfect; practice makes permanent. How you interact with your customers is a habit. You will continue to deal with your customers in the same way until you identify alternate activities and create new habits. The first step in making a change is making an assessment of your current activities.

You are already performing some activities that support each of the principles, but you may not be getting all the results you want. Throughout this chapter, we will identify your habitual activities and which principle these activities can be mapped to. This process should help to identify your weakest and strongest areas in creating loyalty. As you navigate through this process, you should notice that some activities support more than one principle. For example, if your business offers a product warranty that is substantially better than your competitor's, the warranty can be mapped to value and assurance, as well as to differentiation. The warranty is an activity that supports value and assurance, but because it is so far superior to what is offered elsewhere, it is also a differentiator. Every activity you perform has the possibility of serving more than one principle.

Developing Activities That Support People Doing Business With People

Ask yourself these questions: Are you the kind of person people want to do business with? Do you have your customers' best interests in mind? Are you truly interested in your customers? Do you spend more time talking or listening to your customers? Do you make a habit of asking your customers questions? Do you spend most of your time with customers making statements? Do you really know your customers? Do you really understand your customers? Do you lead your customers? Do you help your customers? How are you serving your customers?

It takes character and courage to put your customers' interests above your own. It is much easier to give a sales presentation and then ask for the order than it is to try to understand and lead a customer. It takes character to live by your beliefs. It takes courage to trust in your customer.

People feel important when you respond to them. In a retail store this response is usually no more than a cashier taking a customer's money and hopefully thanking them. Loyalty is created when a deeper, more meaningful response is made. Usually, when a customer arrives at an appliance store or car dealership the salesperson asks, "Can I help you?" or "Can I show you something?" The customer responds with, "I'm just looking," or "I'm interested in a refrigerator," or "I'm interested in a four-door sedan." The salesperson then begins to tout his product and launches into a description of whatever he has to sell. This is nothing more or less than a sales presentation. The salesperson has only demonstrated his ability to recite, not the ability to respond.

When that customer entered the appliance store or car dealership, he brought his entire history with him. He brought every bit of experience he has had with refrigerators or automobiles. He brought every bit of experience he has had in making major purchases. He wants to do business with a person who will recognize and respond to that experience. If the salesperson asks, "What kind of refrigerator do you have now?" or says, "Tell me about the car I saw you driving up in." the customer will be delighted to share his experiences. The specifics of your business aren't important, every customer has either had or not had experience with it. If this is his first car, refrigerator, custom draperies, house, or dining room table he wants you to know about it and respond. If he is an experienced buyer, he wants you to know about that as well. The customer wants you to know so you will respond to his likes and dislikes, good experiences and bad.

When you know what the customer's experiences have been, you begin to know about him. The more you know about him, the more you can respond to him and his experiences.

Doctors and dentists get high marks for learning as much as possible about their patients' health before they attempt to diagnosis problems or prescribe cures. Their procedure is designed to make them responsible. Medical professionals don't tout their education or qualification before they begin their examination: Their attention is focused on the patient. In the waiting room, the patient completes a form asking: vital statistics, the patient's medical history, family medical history, and the purpose of today's visit. Your doctor or dentist will review and discuss this information before they address your current health issue. They are demonstrating an interest in you. They want to know as much about you, as it pertains to your health, as possible. They are dealing with you as an individual, and they are demonstrating your unique importance.

How do you interact with your customers? Do you learn as much as possible about them and their circumstance so you can know, understand, help, and lead them?

As an exercise, write a list of how you deal with a sample customer. Choose a customer you are currently doing business with. Your list should describe everything you do to prepare for your transaction with this customer:

- ✓ Did you make an appointment?
- ✓ Did you research your past transactions with this customer?
- ✓ What did you do to learn additional information about this customer before you met with her?

Your list should include everything that takes place while you are with the customer:

✓ Are you talking or are you listening?

✓ What do you do to indicate the customer's importance?

Your list should include everything you do to follow up with the customer after the transaction is completed:

✓ Did you send a personal thank you note?

✓ Did you call the customer to get their post purchase impressions?

My wife and I recently met Jay, a construction attorney from Indianapolis, at a dinner party. He told us that his firm goes to great expense to entertain its clients. Jay said that his clients appreciated being recognized as important customers. "Sometimes," he said, "clients don't like or want to be entertained. I have a client that represents a substantial and growing part of my practice. I invited this client to a ball game. I had box seats in a luxury suite. The client told me that he didn't do that sort of thing. What do I do in a situation like that?" I told Jay the best way to demonstrate his client's importance is to honor the client's request. Don't invite him to outings or other entertainment venues but do tell him, "I really appreciate your business. The business you do with our firm is growing and has a substantial impact on my success. I'm telling you this so you will know how important you are to me. Thank you for your continuing loyalty."

Your list should note everything you do that tells your customer in words and actions how important they are to you and how well you know and understand them. You are only able to respond to your customer's needs, wants, and desires if you know and understand them. They will notice and appreciate your preparation and dealings with them as an important customer. They will recognize you as a person doing business with them as an important individual.

Ben Knows Who Is Important

Ben Feldman was a legendary insurance agent with New York Life. Ben sold billions of dollars of insurance in his hometown of East Liverpool, Ohio. He was a shy fellow with a slight lisp and not at all what you would picture as a super salesman type. I saw Ben being interviewed at a sales convention. The interviewer asked Ben what his clients thought of him. Ben said, "I guess they would say I'm a little bit of a stinker. They would say I push a little too much. But I push because I care about my customers as people. I care enough about my customers to do my homework. I have carefully asked them questions so I know what they want to accomplish. When I push them, I'm really helping them make a decision." Ben Feldman is no longer with us, but before his death he led New York Life in sales and customer loyalty. Ben understood that people always do business with people. Ben believed every one of his customers were important and worthy of his best effort in knowing, understanding, helping, and leading them.

Developing Activities That Support Differentiation

Ask yourself these questions:

✓ How am I different from my competitors?

✓ Am I more courteous, prompt, professional, personable, or caring than my competitors are?

✓ Besides the product and service, what do my customers expect and always receive from me?

✓ Why would I be the first person someone would think of if he were looking for the products I sell?

✓ How do I decide where and who I will do business with?

✓ What traits and behaviors do I appreciate most in others?

✓ Am I exhibiting those traits and behaviors for my customers?

✓ What are some of the ways I exhibit these traits and behaviors?

✓ Are the things that make me different important to my customers?

✓ How many different techniques do I use in dealing with my customers?

✓ What kinds of things do my customers say about me?

✓ Do they say anything about me? What kinds of things
　 do I want them to say about me?

It takes curiosity and creativity to develop an effective
differentiator. You must have a natural curiosity about your customers and what is important to them. You must also be creative in looking at your enterprise through the eyes of your customers.

When you examine your own buying preferences, you may notice
that a majority of the places and people you trade with do not have
any notable differentiator. You may stop at the same gas station for
coffee every morning.

✓ Is the coffee better?

✓ Is the gas cheaper?

✓ Is there a better selection of donuts?

✓ Does the clerk greet you by name or mention she
　 didn't see you last week?

✓ Do you stop at this specific gas station simply because
　 it is the most convenient on your way to work?

By virtue of its location, every business is most convenient for
some group of people. When that business personalizes and individu-
alizes how they do business, it is broadening their differentiators to
include a larger audience of customers.

Alex owns a plate glass and window company in Cincinnati, Ohio.
When there are storms, particularly hail or wind storms, Alex and his
family ride around downtown and through business districts looking
for broken glass. They make a list of businesses that have damaged
glass as well as other businesses in the adjacent area. The next morning,
Alex and his sales staff make calls to the businesses that sustained
glass damage. They also call the adjacent businesses and their customers in the area to notify them that they will be working in that part
of town. Alex's business is different from other glass companies; they
don't wait to be called. Alex's business is constantly growing with
loyal customers who recognize the difference.

My friend Rob owns a power washing business in the Midwest.
His company power washes the exterior of hundreds of houses each
year. Rob instructs his workers to always find something extra to wash

after work on the house is completed. Lawn furniture, patios, and sideways are just a few of the things Rob's workers clean at no extra charge. Customers appreciate the additional effort and tell their friends and neighbors. Rob's customers call him year after year to come back and clean their houses. His business continues to grow with loyal customers. This little difference makes a big difference to Rob's customers.

Most major airlines offer frequent flyer miles and discounts through a variety of online travel agencies. Because most airlines offer these benefits, passengers don't perceive much difference and just expect frequent flyer miles and discounts. Southwest and Jet Blue are two notable exceptions. These airlines do all of their own ticketing. In addition, neither airline offers frequent flyer miles. In a marketplace where nearly every major airline is loosing money or barely breaking even, Southwest and Jet Blue are making a profit. The passenger airline business is very complex and there are many more issues involved in profit and loss than just discounting and frequent flyer miles. However, Southwest and Jet Blue are considered unique carriers and both enjoy tremendous loyalty.

Many times a differentiator has little to do with a product or how it is sold. A business can differentiate by appealing to customers' values. Customers don't buy products just because they share values with a business, but if they are already going to buy a competing product, this value agreement can be a strong differentiator.

The Ice Cream Isn't the Only Difference

Ben Cohen and Jerry Greenfield started Ben and Jerry's ice cream manufacturing in an old Burlington, Vermont, gas station in 1978. Twenty years later the business had 700 employees, 132 scoop shops across the United States, and revenues in excess of $160 million. Much of this success is attributable to Ben and Jerry's fiercely loyal customers and employees. Is Ben and Jerry's ice cream that much better than any of their competitors? Maybe, but Ben and Jerry's has also differentiated the company from all its competitors by being what Ben Cohen refers to as a "value-led company." In the book *Ben & Jerry's: The Inside Scoop: How Two Real Guys Built a Business With a Social Conscience and a Sense of Humor* by Fred "Chico" Lager and Jerry Greenfield, Ben is quoted, "When you are a values-led company you're trying to help the community. And when you're try-ing to help the community, people want to buy from you. They want to work for you. They feel invested in your success." Ben and Jerry's uses its ice cream cartons as billboards for social messages. The com-pany is operated in a manner believed to improve the human condition. Through its values-led philosophy, Ben and Jerry's has differentiated itself from all other ice cream companies. This differentiation has little to do with ice cream and everything to do with providing a prod-uct with a differentiator.

As an exercise, choose a customer you have recently transacted business with and who has done business with you on a repeat basis. Make a list noting every detail of your last transaction with this customer. What prompted this last transaction? Did this customer shop or compare your services with a competitor? Why did this cus-tomer ultimately choose your business? Make a list denoting how your business is different from your competitors. Is each of these differ-ences perceived by your customers? Can you advertise or promote these differences? How do these differentiators relate to value and assurance for your customers?

Developing Activities That Support Value and Assurance

Ask yourself these questions:

✓ What do my customers value in doing business with me?

✓ How do I know what is of value to my customers?

✓ How much emphasis do I put on the price of the products that I sell?

✓ Is price really the most important issue to my customers?

✓ Have I asked my customers what is most important to them?

✓ Besides price and product, what other value do I offer my customers?

✓ Do my customers know about these other values?

✓ Do I regularly make promises to my customers?

✓ Do I always keep my promises?

✓ Do I always do what I say I'll do, when I say I'll do it?

✓ Does doing business with me make my customers feel good?

It takes severe objectivity and tremendous tenacity to consistently deliver value and assurance to your customers. Few business owners or professionals would admit that their product or service lacked value or was only equal to other products or services in the marketplace.

All of us believe that what we offer to the world is of value. But in order to deliver value that will create loyal customers, we must be totally objective in the appraisal of the product or service we offer. We must force ourselves to look at our business through the eyes of the customer. Value isn't about words or slogans, it's about making customers feel good, solving their problems, providing the best alternative, and delivering it all with the assurance that they can depend on you.

While you must look at your customers and the marketplace with total objectivity, your customers are viewing products and the marketplace with total subjectivity. The value of goods and services is personal. The customer ultimately decides what something is worth. It is our job to understand what the customer most values and respond appropriately.

The marketplace is dynamic with new products, businesses, services, and ideas being offered every day. Value is not static; it changes as the marketplace changes. Every executive, business owner, entrepreneur, professional, and salesperson needs to be aware and prepared to adapt the value they offer their customers. Assessing what our customers value is an ongoing process and we must be tenacious in our efforts.

IBM was losing its market share in the early 1990s. Its customers believed that IBM offered great products and services, but felt the company was difficult to deal with. Customers complained that communicating with IBM was slow and tedious. Answers to customer's questions often took weeks instead of hours or days. Customers complained that IBM had an attitude of being the only solution to any IT problem. Even when customers requested a different account representative to call on them, IBM sales management refused to assign a new representative. Many of IBM's previously loyal customers began shopping elsewhere. IBM had quality products, but its customers failed to see the value in dealing with a business with a company that seemed so inflexible and difficult.

IBM was objective in its assessment of customer complaints. The company didn't try to defend its behavior, but instead looked for real solutions to improving its relationship with customers. IBM understood that customers have the final say in how they want to be treated and what is of value. IBM regained its market share. IBM is tenacious in its commitment to serving its customers.

It's Not a Motorcycle, It's a Harley

William S. Harley and Arthur Davidson built their first motorcycle in 1903. That first year they only sold one motorcycle. By 1910, the Harley-Davidson Motor Company was up and running and sold 3,200 bikes. By 1920, the company saw its production exceed 28,000 motorcycles. Over the years the company has had more than its share of problems. The company suffered from a reputation for poor quality and approached bankruptcy on more than one occasion. The company has had to compete from an unfair disadvantage against foreign competitors that have much lower labor rates.

Today, Harley-Davidson enjoys a tremendous reputation for quality and value. It not only competes, but also dominates the large motorcycle marketplace. The motorcycles the company competes against are substantially less expensive and outperform the Harley in speed and economy. How does Harley-Davidson do it?

The Harley-Davidson relationship with cyclists is one difference between it and its competitors. Harley-Davidson's customers aren't just buying a motorcycle, they are buying the Harley experience.

The experience is more than just riding a motorcycle. The experience includes membership in the Harley Owners Group, or HOGs, which has local chapters throughout America. The National organization as well as the local chapters host open houses, schedule motorcyclist vacations, and even offer support groups specifically for female riders.

The sale of Harley accessories, including riding leathers, T-shirts, key chains, and other items are reported to represent a substantial portion of the company's revenue, and these products further define the Harley experience. Harley owners could buy these items at less cost from several retailers, but their loyalty requires them to buy authentic Harley-Davidson goods.

Harley-Davidson doesn't just sell a motorcycle, it sells an experience, a culture, and value. Harley-Davidson assures this value by offering parts and service on all their motorcycles, regardless of the model or age.

Harley-Davidson offers a unique value proposition: the total experience of Harley-Davidson motorcycle ownership. It is more than a fraternity, it is a brotherhood. The only brand of motorcycle that can give you entrance into this brotherhood is Harley-Davidson. The year or model does not matter; if it's a Harley, you're in.

As an exercise, choose a few of your current customers who you deal with on a repeat basis. Ask them what they most value in your products, services, and the way you do business. Ask them with whom they would do business if they weren't trading with you. Ask them what they like about this other business. Ask them what they would change about your business. Repeat this exercise with new customers or prospects that have not done business with you. Does your value proposition support the responses you are getting? Can you adapt your value proposition to better serve your customers?

Developing Activities That Support Effective Communication

Ask yourself these questions:
- ✓ Do I thank my customers for their business?
- ✓ How do I thank my customers?
- ✓ How often do I thank my customers?
- ✓ How often do I contact my customers?
- ✓ What do I tell them?
- ✓ Are my communications with my customers different than my communications with non-customers?

✓ Can my customers tell that I treat them differently?

✓ How can they tell?

✓ Do my communications recognize the importance of my customers?

✓ How frequently do my customers hear from me?

✓ Do I make my customers feel special, like "insiders"?

✓ What do I do to make them feel special?

It takes a sincere interest in your customers and a willing dedication to effectively communicate. You will create customer loyalty when you communicate effectively before, during, and after business transactions. People detect sincerity. Customers know if you truly have an interest in them. They can tell if your interest is in the sale or in them. Your sincere interest in the customer is reflected through your communications during transactions. Your willing dedication to establishing a relationship before transacting business and consistently following up after business transaction demonstrates that you are effectively communicating.

The average American business loses half of its customers every five years. You have to do something different than what the average business does if you are going to avoid this loss. The average business owner or sales professional is typically very effective in closing a sale while they are transacting business or in a sales presentation; however, these same business owners and sales professionals do little to build relationships before or after transacting business. This void is your opportunity to stand out from your competition.

Your first opportunity comes before you transact or attempt to close a business deal. Remember, we are talking about customers who have already done business with you. The homework or preparation you do before you meet with the customer demonstrates your interest. If you are well prepared, you are telling the customer they are important. Even if your only effort is to become familiar with their past transactions, you are demonstrating your interest. The more preparation you do, the more appreciative your customer will be.

Your second opportunity to stand out from the competition is when you talk with your customer. When you think about your own buying experiences, how often does it appear that the people you are doing business with are most interested in making a sale today. The message usually seems to be: what would it take to get you to buy this car, house, copier, subscription, insurance, or whatever today? Sometimes the message takes the form of, "If you were renewing your contract today, would you?" Sales managers encourage their sales staff to use these kinds of closing questions. When the salesperson is asking these questions, the customers is hearing, "It's not about you, it's about a sale. I'm not thinking about you, I'm thinking about the money. We'll worry about loyalty next time, right now I'm trying to earn a living." Put yourself in the customer's position. Help them make a decision, don't force them to make a decision. Don't push them; lead them to the best possible solution.

The third opportunity to effectively communicate with your customer comes after you have transacted business. Are you thanking your customer for their business? Is your thank you sincere? Are you sending a thank you note to provide tangible evidence of your appreciation? Are you communicating with your customers with newsletters or e-zines?

Maintaining contact with your customers after you have done business with them requires dedication. You must develop a system of routine, regular, and frequent contacts. Newsletters, if they are personalized, can be very effective. A personalized newsletter is a newsletter that talks about people. It talks about you, your staff, or about your customers.

Newsletters or notices that only announce upcoming sales or new products are perceived by customers to be no more than advertisements. When these same messages are personalized, the results improve dramatically. A poorly written but highly personalized communication will produce greater results than a beautifully written impersonal communication. People want to do business with people, and your communications after the sale should serve this purpose.

This Stockbroker Keeps in Touch

Dick Wilson is vice president at UBS Financial Services and has been a very successful stockbroker with a six-figure income for nearly 25 years. Dick didn't come from the right family or the right side of town or have any special privilege before becoming a stockbroker. Dick came from a military family and spent his youth moving from military base to military base. Dick was not endowed with social connections and, in fact, didn't have any base of business at all when he started. Dick got most of his prospects from other stockbrokers who were leaving the business. The guy leaving might have a couple of dozen clients or prospects. Dick would ask the guy, "Hey, do you mind if I call on your clients after you leave?"

Dick claims his success is due to his enormous amount of client contact. He makes 25,000 phone calls every year. That is not a misprint. None of those calls are cold calls: Dick is calling clients and people referred from his clientele. Dick reports it's not that difficult to make 25,000 phone calls per year. In fact, he says, "It is simple. Make 500 calls per week. That's 100 calls a day. Even if you only work eight hours, that's only 12 calls an hour." His average call is three minutes, so he still has about 20 minutes every hour to do other things.

The part that's best about Dick's activities is his good use of time. Dick was probably the first sales executive I ever saw using a headset. Since he does not have to hold the phone, his hands are free to address envelopes and write notes while he is talking to his clients. Dick is sending stuff—thank you notes, prospectuses, and newspaper clippings—to his clients constantly. Dick even saves his junk mail and resends it to his clients who might have an interest in whatever was sent to him. Dick knows his greatest sales tool is staying in touch with his clients. He continually lets them know he is interested in them and how important they are to him.

As an exercise, choose three or four sample customers. These should be customers who you have dealt with on a repeat basis. Make a list of the work and time you spent preparing before the last transaction with each of these people. The way some businesses operate, you may not be able to prepare before you meet with a customer. If this is your situation, how much time and effort did you spend reviewing prior dealings with these customers before you began transacting current business?

Examine your style of speech while you were transacting business with these sample customers. Were you most interested in helping them or closing a sale? Was closing the sale most important for you or for them? You may want to record a few meetings with your customers so you can review and evaluate what your customers are hearing.

Make a list of all correspondence, newsletters, phone calls, thank you notes, or any other contact you had with these customers since their last transaction. Are you routinely, regularly, and frequently contacting your customers? Is your contact personalized?

Developing Activities That Support Focus

Ask yourself these questions:

✓ How do I define success?

✓ At what point can I proclaim myself successful?

✓ Is my success tied to the accomplishment of a goal?

✓ Is my success defined as progress toward the continuing development of a relationship?

✓ Am I more interested in new customers or furthering the relationship with each of my existing customers?

✓ How am I currently demonstrating my desire to develop loyal customers?

✓ Do I think of and treat the people I do business with as loyal customers?

✓ What evidence do my customers have of my belief in their loyalty?

✓ Do my actions support my beliefs?

The law of life is the law of expectation. You don't always get what you want, but you do always get what you truly expect. Your thoughts and actions support your truest beliefs. We think we must have loyal customers first, but the truth is that we must believe before we see. Are you doing those things that bolster your belief, or are you waiting to see loyal customers first?

The external world we see does not cause us to think or act a certain way. Instead, the external world we see is a product of our internal thinking. Our thinking becomes objectified. What we think becomes our reality: It is our thinking that causes our external world. No matter what is taking place in the world today, it started as a thought in someone's mind. The external world is an effect; our thinking is the cause. What we think causes the effect we see. You can change how you think about your business and your customers at this very moment, and your thinking will cause a change. The effect of your thinking will be whatever you truly believe. Your deepest beliefs determine your expectations. Remember, the law of life is the law of expectation.

When you believe in the value and abundance of loyal customers, all of your actions will support this belief. You will think about and treat your customers as loyal. You will conduct your business with them as individuals, as people doing business with people. They will recognize their importance through your behavior. Your business will be perceived as different because it is different. Your products have value and you offer assurances. Your customers appreciate your value proposition and are assured they are doing business with the right people. You communicate effectively with your customers. Your customers recognize your interest and sincerity and feel like they are an integral part of your business. Your concentration is focused on your loyal customers. Your business is committed to creating loyalty. Your customers understand your commitment and freely recommend you to their families, friends, and business associates.

State Farm Focuses on Its Loyal Customers

On August 24, 1992, hurricane Andrew made landfall on the southern-most tip of Florida. Andrew accounted for 43 deaths and the destruction of 86,000 single-family homes. The estimated damage from Andrew was $16 billion. The resulting insurance claims caused several small insurers to go out of business. Several large insurers paid their claims and discontinued selling insurance in Florida. They felt the cost of doing business in a hurricane-prone area was too great.

State Farm Insurance Company also suffered substantial losses, but instead of paying its claims and retracting from the area, State Farm made a further commitment to its Florida policyholders. State Farm felt it had spent a lot of time and money developing a base of loyal customers and it did not want to give up its most valuable asset. Not only did State Farm continue coverage for victims of hurricane Andrew, it paid more in claims than it was required to. Many of

State Farm's policyholders suffered wind damage to the roofs of their homes. Houses built prior to Hurricane Andrew did not have to meet government Hurricane Standards. State Farm gave its policyholders additional funds, in many cases more than $1000 additional, to make their homes comply with the new Hurricane Standards for roofing. State Farm reasoned that it would stay in the Florida marketplace and would benefit from insuring homes that were safer. State Farm clearly focused on building and maintaining relationships that create loyalty.

Trish works in sales at a radio station in California. She is consistently the number-one salesperson at her station. Most of the other salespeople spend a substantial portion of each day prospecting for new advertisers, but Trish seldom prospects. Her day is filled with dealing with loyal customers.

Trish began her advertising career to support herself while she was attending the University of Southern California. She started at the station the summer after completing her sophomore year. The money was good and she loved her job.

Trish hated prospecting but she loved working with the few clients the station had assigned her. Instead of making phone calls and stopping in to see prospects, Trish spent all her time catering to the few existing customers she had. She reviewed her clients' current and historic advertising schedules. She compared the advertising fees these businesses were paying to the results they were getting. She was totally committed to helping these businesses maximize the results from advertising on her station. She never thought about a client canceling its advertising. All of her thoughts were on improving results. Trish thought of herself as her client's partner in a mutual quest to grow its business through advertising.

Many times Trish was able to reduce the amount a customer was spending on advertising while increasing the results. Better-written and better-produced advertising brought more business to her clients. Careful scheduling of advertisements for specific target audiences allowed her clients to reduce the amount of ads while increasing traffic to their businesses. Trish's clients loved her: They appreciated the work she did and they loved to recommend Trish to their business friends and associates. Trish has never had to prospect because her loyal customers are prospecting for her every day. Trish never returned to the University of Southern California because she was making too much money and would have hated to leave her customers.

As an exercise, examine your thoughts about new customers. How much effort and time do you spend on prospecting or otherwise trying to attract new customers? If given a choice, do you give preferential treatment to new customers? Do first-time buyers get a discount or incentive? Do you receive an incentive or additional compensation for bringing in new customers?

Examine your thoughts about repeat customers. Do you recognize each of the three benefits of loyal customers (cost of attraction, ease of doing business, and predictability) when you are dealing with a repeat customer? Are you using each of these benefits to maximize your productivity? Loyal customers are predictable. They buy your product or service on a repeat basis. Are you using this predictability to prepare for their next purchase? Are you using this predictability to help them schedule their next purchase or their next meeting with you? Loyal customers are easier to do business with because you are familiar with them and what they want. Are you using this familiarity and the history of your relationship to make every transaction better and more efficient than the last? Loyal customers are already doing business with you; you do not have a cost in time or money to attract these customers. Do you recognize these savings in evaluating your profitability?

As you examine the benefits and commit to focusing on loyal customers, you are reinforcing your beliefs. You are setting your expectations.

Mapping Activities

As a final exercise, make a list of your daily work activities. Your list should include everything you do from the time you arrive at work until you leave. You may want to categorize your day into 15-minute segments. What do you do during your first 15 minutes at work? Do you check your e-mail? Do you retrieve voice mail messages? Do you go to a job site? Make a list of your activities for an entire day.

Map each activity of your workday to one of the five principles that create loyalty. Some of your activities won't support a principle, but many will. Just answering or responding to an e-mail may not map back to a principle; however, if you differentiate yourself by answering every e-mail within one hour or one day, then answering an e-mail could be mapped to differentiation. Responding to voice mail may not map back to a principle; however, if you use every phone conversation with your customers to substantiate people doing business with people, then map this activity to that principle. Map every activity of your workday to one of the principles.

After you have completed this exercise you will find that you support some principles more than others. For example, many of your activities may support the principle of effective communication, but you may be doing less to support the principle of value and assurance. When I work with a business and we use this exercise, we invariably discover one predominant principle that is being ignored. This one principle then becomes our target and we develop activities to support this principle.

Identifying a Predominant Lack

Dr. Hall is the president and founder of Northwest Pathology Associates, a medium-sized pathology lab in the state of Washington. Dr. Hall began this medical practice nearly 15 years ago. Today there are nine board-certified pathologists in Dr. Hall's group. Each of these doctors is an equal partner in the practice. The business also employs six lab technicians, four administrative assistants, and an office manager.

Northwest Pathology Associates provides laboratory services to other doctors and medical clinics in the area. Because this practice does not have any patients of their own, Northwest Pathology Associates is totally dependent on other doctors in the community for work. Its customers are not the patients, they are the doctors who send specimens and tissue samples to the lab for testing.

Northwest Pathology Associates uses only the most modern and up-to-date equipment and practices. Because of its location and competition, this group offers the quickest turnaround times on all lab studies.

Unfortunately, while the community it operates in has grown, this pathology practice has seen little or no increase in revenue over the last few years.

When I first met with Dr. Hall and his associates, I found a well-run medical practice and office. The office staff kept accurate records of every lab test that was conducted, including the results as well as when they received the specimen and when the results were returned to the attending physician. All the work that came into the lab was immediately tested and then assigned to a pathologist. The pathologist would study the lab results and then complete a report. The pathologist assigned to study any given lab report was random. On a given day, an attending physician might receive three or four reports from three or four different doctors at Northwest Pathology Associates.

My initial study of this business also disclosed that there were a total of 300 doctors in the area that might use Northwest Pathology Associates. Most of these doctors were using Dr. Hall's group for some of their pathology work, but few were using the firm exclusively.

We matched the activities of Northwest Pathology Associates to the five principles that create customer loyalty. This lab was differentiated by virtue of being the only local lab. Its value proposition was the fastest turnaround time on lab reports. It assured its customers of accuracy by having two pathologists read the results from every lab test. It effectively communicated with its customers through the detailed diagnosis outlined in each lab report. It was focused on its existing customers. It recognized the 300 local physicians as its entire universe of customers: All of its focus was on this group of doctors.

The one principle Dr. Hall's group had ignored was: *people do business with people*. These doctors were providing a superior service but spent no time in developing relationships with the referring physicians who were providing them with all their work.

There were some things we could do to improve or increase the activities that support each principle, but our predominant interest was in giving attention to the principle *people do business with people*.

Dr. Hall's office manager subdivided the firm's clientele and made each doctor responsible for approximately 30 clients. All lab reports and other correspondence to a client doctor would come from the same pathologist. In addition, the pathologists made quarterly phone calls or visited in person with their assigned client doctors. The intent of these visits was to thank their clients for their business and ask how they might improve their service.

Northwest Pathology Associates began sending a quarterly newsletter to the office of each of its client doctors. Each newsletter has a feature story about a lab technician or one of the pathologists. These stories are biographical in nature and many times describe a hunting trip or interests in a sport or hobby. The newsletters contain a technical report on a new procedure or a piece of equipment used in the lab. A regular feature is an ongoing tabulation of average turnaround times for lab reports. The newsletter is also a great way to introduce new services.

Northwest Pathology Associates's newsletter is an effective way to communicate. The newsletter supports the principle of effective communication; however, the newsletter's most important function is to support the principle of people do business with people. By sharing personal stories and the experiences of doctors and the staff, customers are learning who they are doing business with.

The point is that activities that support one principle may, in fact, support several principles. The newsletter supports effective communication, but it also reinforces the firm's value proposition, differentiates, and demonstrates people do business with people.

Since embarking on a mission of creating customer loyalty, Northwest Pathology Associates has seen its revenue and profit increase each year.

Summary

✓ Loyalty is created one customer at a time. You are the only person that can create loyalty with your customers. There are thousands of things you can do to create customer satisfaction, but there are only five principles you must support to create create loyalty. I am suggesting you incorporate the five principles that create loyalty into your daily work efforts. Your rewards will be enormous.

✓ Include other members of your company, staff, team, or department in this endeavor. When others are included, each of you will strengthen your resolve and benefit from ideas generated by the group. You will also benefit from the objectivity of your peers as you assess and develop specific activities.

✓ Your initial assessment and the mapping of your current activities to the loyalty principles may take several hours. This process can be enhanced if you meet once a week with your peers and only assess and map one principle per week. Even while you are completing these initial meetings, by the third or fourth meeting you should have progress to report in your quest for loyalty.

✓ Creating loyalty is a journey that you will never complete. The results from your efforts will inspire you and your peers with new ideas and activities to further develop. Every business has its own personality, peculiarities, attributes, and characteristics, so as you and your peers develop your specific activities, you will be writing the standard for creating loyalty in your specific business.

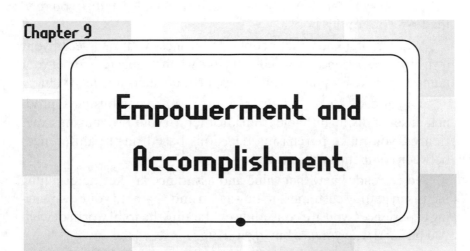

Chapter 9

Empowerment and Accomplishment

The secret to success is constancy of purpose.
—Benjamin Disraeli, former
prime minister of England

In the previous chapters, we discussed the benefits of customer loyalty, the five principles that create loyalty, and how you can apply this information to your business. The five principles are truths: They don't work just sometimes for some people; they are working for you or against you all the time. The five principles are like gravity; gravity is on all of the time. You don't have to know about gravity or understand it for it to affect you. You do not have to know about or understand the five principles of customer loyalty to have them affect your business. Your business is prospering from the abundance or suffering from the lack of loyal customers right now. The five principles are affecting your business whether you acknowledge them or not.

Application of Intuitive Knowledge

Having read this far, you know why customers come back. You understand the five principles of customer loyalty. On an intuitive basis, I believe you were familiar with each of the principles before you read the first word of this book.

You already knew that people do business with people. In your own buying experiences, you feel a kinship when people remember your name and make it a point to know, understand, help, and lead you.

You already knew that differentiators make one business, product, or seller distinguishable from another. In your own buying experiences, you make purchasing decisions based on the differences between competing alternatives.

You already knew that value and assurance are key determining factors in getting customers to buy again and again. In your own buying experiences, you are constantly evaluating the total worth of what you buy and who you are buying it from.

You already knew that effective communication was listening, learning, and responding. In your own buying experiences, you reward those people that talk straight, develop an ongoing dialogue, and are constantly listening to you.

You already knew that little could be accomplished unless sufficient focus is directed to the problem or opportunity. In your own business purchasing experiences, you appreciate and reward those who focus their attention on your specific wants, needs, and desires.

You may have intuitively known the five principles, but you may not have applied them in your business endeavors. On a day-to-day basis, every business is bombarded with challenges. How you define your challenges and what actions you take determine how successful you will be. A mission statement can help you undertake this task. A mission statement begins with the end result in mind and clearly defines a goal so that daily activity will lead to the right conclusion.

Lesson From the Military

Ted is a retired military colonel who spent 25 years in the intelligence branch of the U.S. Marine Corp. Ted is a history buff and finds comfort in understanding the world today by understanding the world of yesterday. Today, Ted works in the training and education department of a major corporation.

Ted attends most of the conventions and general sales meetings of the company for which he works. He shared with me that he was attending a convention and was in the hotel lounge one evening when a couple of his colleagues were discussing the current state of their company. All of these fellows were in agreement that the company seemed to be forever changing marketing plans, target audiences, and generally how the company conducts its business. Ted's colleagues were young fellows in their 30s and held management jobs at the junior executive level. While they had worked at the company for only a couple years they each admitted that the company seemed to radically change its direction too frequently.

What is the mission?

Ted asked his colleagues, "What do you think the mission of our company should be?" The young executives responded with lengthy manifestos that described markets, products, and competitive position.

Ted told them, "You fellows are too young to remember, but World War II was the greatest endeavor of mankind. It employed more people, resources, and money than any other endeavor before or since. The outcome of World War II would determine the future of the world. Do you know the mission statement for World War II?" he asked. Neither of the young men knew the answer.

Ted continued, "The mission statement for World War II was just two words: *unconditional surrender*. The strategy was *Europe first*. The tactics to be used were *land*, *air*, and *sea*. In order for a mission to be successful, it has to be clear and easily understood by everyone involved. If the mission of World War II was as complex as the mission statements you just offered, we would still be fighting the war. The war effort included everyone. It wasn't just soldiers that fought the war. Every American was involved. People participated in the Civil Air Patrol, endured rationing, and volunteered for all kinds of activities that supported the war effort. Their understanding of the mission was critical to the success of the war. A mission statement should guide everyone involved."

Do you have a mission statement for your business? Is it three pages or three words? Does everyone in your company understand the mission?

Today there is a prevailing belief that the purpose of every business is to earn a profit. This belief is pervasive as well as prevailing. Most people believe profit is the most important function of any business. This belief is widely accepted, but may not be as relevant as you might think.

Ford's Purpose of Business

Henry Ford's life was filled with accomplishments and contradictions. He was an odd fellow in many ways, but he really changed the world by putting it on wheels. Ford used his company as a sort of social laboratory. He adopted a paternal policy to reform his workers' lives both at home and at work. He felt it was his obligation to help improve the human condition.

In 1914, Ford announced his plan to share the Ford Motor Company's profits with workers, paying them $5 for an eight-hour shift. Five bucks doesn't sound like much money today, but at that time a man earning $5 a day could support his family in relative comfort. Five dollars a day was enough money to put food on the table, pay the rent, and set aside a little bit each week toward the purchase of a car. The workers' ability to set aside a little bit each week toward the purchase of cars was the most important issue to Ford. Ford knew that if the typical worker could afford a car, the Ford Motor Company and the entire world would do just fine. Henry Ford's guiding philosophy was "The purpose of commerce is to provide jobs. A by-product of commerce is profit to a company's owners."

Ford reasoned that if he had all the money in the world, it would not matter one wit if there were no goods or services to purchase. When commerce creates jobs, it also creates consumers. Consumers make the economy and the world go round.

The Boy Scouts of America was incorporated in 1910 with the purpose of building character and physical fitness in young men. Incentives for being a Boy Scout include camping trips, merit badges, and friendship. A camping trip is an incentive, it is not the purpose. Merit badges and friendship are also incentives to being a Boy Scout, they are not the purpose.

The purpose of commerce in any society is the creation of jobs. Without jobs there are no consumers; without consumers, there is no commerce. Every business is a part of the tapestry of commerce, and profit is an incentive of commerce.

Many businesses today operate for the sole purpose of earning a profit to distribute to their investors or stockholders. These businesses reason that the investors, as owners of the enterprise, are entitled to a profit. They believe that profit is not an incentive, it is the purpose. They are saying that there is no other reason to invest in a company other than the belief that a profit will be earned. This view does not fairly recognize all the stakeholders in a business or the value of organizational loyalty.

Stakeholders

Investors, employees, customers, and the community at large are all stakeholders. Investors are stakeholders because of their monetary contribution. In exchange for their investment, they own some part of the enterprise. They have a capital, or equity, stake in the business. The value of their equity may go up or down in value based on the marketplace and how well the company performs. The performance of the company may also generate income for the investor from profit.

Customers are stakeholders; they also invest in the enterprise. The amount of money they invest is often larger than that of the investor. The customer who buys an automobile is investing more than the typical stockholder. If the automobile is faulty and proves dangerous, the customer has more at risk than the investor.

Employees are stakeholders. Employees invest their time, effort, education, and skill in the business. They invest their careers. Layoffs, downsizing, and relocation are just a few of the risks employees take when they invest their careers with a business. Over the course of history, many employees have sacrificed their lives in their pursuit of employment. Black lung and plant accidents are just a few of the tragedies and risks of the workplace.

Businesses operate in communities. These communities, whether they are villages, towns, or cities, are also stakeholders. Municipalities provide streets and roads, water and power utilities, as well as police and fire protection. These communities provide schools to educate and train workers. The citizens of these municipalities pay for this infrastructure through their tax dollars. Communities are stakeholders because they have also invested in these hometown businesses.

Businesses that are incorporated enjoy special privileges. The federal government provides for special tax treatment for corporations. Corporations, unlike sole proprietors and partnerships, continue on after their owners die, in effect, giving the business perpetual life. The national government is a stakeholder.

Why Invest Without a Profit Motive?

You may find this notion of profit as an incentive rather than a purpose foreign to your thinking. You may believe the only stakeholder who is entitled is the stockholder. Are you wondering why someone would invest without a profit motive? Is the creation of jobs too philosophical when you are worried about your own well-being?

I am not advocating that investors should invest in any business that will not offer a return for their investment. I am not suggesting that businesses can lure investors without a profit incentive. To the contrary, I am suggesting investors should invest where there are substantial opportunities for gain. However, the greatest opportunity lies with companies that embrace organizational loyalty. Organizational loyalty recognizes all stakeholders. Organizational loyalty recognizes investors, employees, and customers as stakeholders of the enterprise.

Malden Mills

Malden Mills is a textile mill based in Lawrence, Massachusetts. The mill was founded in 1906 by the grandfather of current owner, Aaron Feuerstein. A fire destroyed three of the 10 buildings on its complex on December 11, 1995.

The mill employed 3,000 workers and was the only industry of any size in Lawrence. Most of the workers believed they had lost their jobs forever when the mill burned down, but Aaron Feuerstein, CEO, believed differently.

Feuerstein told his employees, "Your dedication and hard work are what have made Malden Mills successful. The township of Lawrence has supported Malden Mills for many years and Malden Mills is not going to turn its back on Lawrence."

While the mill was being rebuilt and equipment was being moved to restart production, the company continued salaries and benefits to all 3,000 of its workers. During this period, the township of Lawrence remained vibrant. Businesses, churches, and schools remained open and families stayed together in Lawrence.

Malden Mills is the sole producer of Polartec and Polarfleece synthetic fabrics and various other upholstery fabrics. By the time the company returned to full production, it had lost substantial market share to foreign competitors with much lower operating costs. Malden Mills struggled and finally filed for reorganizational bankruptcy.

Critics and creditors of Malden Mills questioned Feuerstein's charity to his workers. They charged that Feuerstein was too charitable and not prudent enough when he continued the workers' wages after the fire. Feuerstein believes his workers are an asset, not an expense. He believes he has a responsibility to all stakeholders and it would be unconscionable to put 3,000 workers on the streets. Feuerstein said, "Maybe on paper our company is worth less to Wall Street, but I can tell you that it's worth more. We're doing fine."

Feuerstein did not waste the millions of dollars he spent in continuing wages after the fire. It was not just an act of generosity or charity, it was well reasoned and sound to invest millions of dollars in Malden Mills' most critical asset. Continuing wages to laid off workers was an investment. Malden Mills' CEO, Feuerstein, is a striking contrast to the CEOs of other companies who earn enormous salaries by eliminating jobs and moving plants to countries with minimal labor rates.

At the bankruptcy hearing, all but one creditor believed Malden Mills could emerge successful. All the creditors but one believed in Feuerstein and his evaluation of the worth of his workers. The one dissenting creditor wanted his money right then. He disagreed with Feuerstein's actions and charged him with spending someone else's money. On the courthouse steps, Aaron Feuerstein said, "I did what was right. I did the morally correct thing to do…and I would do it again."

Today, Malden Mills is a vibrant company: It is producing more Polartec and Polarfleece than ever before and has emerged from bankruptcy and is more profitable than ever. The township of Lawrence is vibrant. The workers at Malden Mills are committed because they understand that loyalty works both ways.

Commitment to a Mission

Tom Monaghan and his brother James borrowed $500 to purchase DomiNick's pizza store in Ypsilanti, Michigan, in 1960. After one year in business, James had all he wanted of the pizza business and traded his ownership in the store for his brother's used Volkswagen Beetle.

As the sole owner of the struggling business, Tom changed the name of the store to Domino's Pizza in 1965. By 1967, business had improved and the company opened its first franchise store. Over the next 17 years Domino's Pizza grew to include 2,841 stores and became the fastest growing pizza company in the United States. Today, Domino's Pizza operates more than 7,000 stores including more than 2,000 stores outside the United States. Its worldwide revenue exceeds $3.5 billion and the company is still growing at a remarkable pace.

Tom Monaghan developed and nurtured his business on the vision:

"Exceptional people on a mission to be the best pizza delivery company in the world utilizing the company's guiding principles, which are:

1. We demand integrity.
2. Our people come first.
3. We take great care of our customers.
4. We make 'Perfect 10' pizzas every day.
5. We operate with smart hustle and positive energy."

Domino's Pizza starts with regular people and teaches them to be exceptional through teamwork and the company's vision. Its vision/mission statement recognizes daily activities as the path to accomplishment. Domino's puts its team members first with the imperative, "Our people come first."

Does Domino's have a profit motive? Of course they do. But it is interesting to note that profit is an incentive of its success, it is not the purpose. Its purpose is clearly, "To be the best pizza delivery business in the world." They measure being the best by the five principles that guide them. These are not just words on a piece on paper; Domino's has lived by these principles.

Domino's has demonstrated this very real concern for making its 140,000 team members its number one priority. Domino's assists its team members in times of special need or tragedy as a result of natural disasters, unexpected afflictions, on-the-job accidents, and other emergencies. Domino's Partners Foundation was founded in 1986 and has helped thousands of team members and their families with financial, emotional, intermediary, and advisory assistance.

Domino's has also demonstrated its very real concern for taking great care of its customers through participation in many community and charitable organizations where its employees and customers live. The company has a Pizza Donation program through the Community Relations Department. Domino's stores in New York City and Washington, D.C., provided more than 12,000 pizzas to relief workers at Ground Zero following the September 11, 2001, tragedy. Domino's established a team member matching funds program to financially assist the American Red Cross and donated $350,000 to the Disaster Relief Effort.

In July 2001, Domino's Pizza began a long-term national partnership with the Make-A-Wish Foundation. Through this alliance, the company is dedicated to delivering wishes to children with life-threatening illnesses.

Many companies helped during the September 11 tragedy and many companies are philanthropic; however, Domino's has made it an integral part of its mission. It is the purpose of its business.

In 2002, Tom Monaghan founded Ave Maria University. He announced he was donating $200 million to this cause. Ave Maria is the first Catholic university to be built in the United States in 40 years. The campus is being built on agricultural land in Collier County, Florida, in the southwestern part of the state. The campus is scheduled to be completed in 2006.

Within just a few years, Ave Maria University will be the centerpiece of a college town. There will be apartment buildings, single-family neighborhoods, shopping centers, restaurants, medical offices, insurance agencies, barbershops, and enterprises of all sorts. No one is sure exactly what the town of Ave Maria will look like, but public officials are claiming that the town will have a population of about 50,000 within 10 years.

Back in 1961, when Tom Monaghan handed his brother James the keys to his Volkswagen Beetle, I doubt that he considered the problems or opportunities of founding a university and a town. But then again, the purpose of his business was to do just that.

The purpose of a business or the incentives that may be derived seldom come to fruition in a year, or even several years. However, any business with a worthwhile purpose can be immediately successful. (See Chapter 7 for "What Is Your Definition of Success?") The purpose of any business must be addressed every day. This purpose must be a constant in every endeavor the business attempts. Aristotle said that you can change things only if they lie steady under your hand. Constancy of purpose is the appropriate starting point for every business enterprise. Without a constancy of purpose, the variables of the marketplace will strip a business of its aim. Like a ship without a rudder, the business will be powerless to reach any worthwhile destination.

The business management guru Peter Drucker said, "The purpose of every business is to get and keep customers." I wonder if the CEOs of IBM or AT&T considered Drucker's advice when they laid off 100,000 and 44,000 workers, respectively. These layoffs took place during the 1990s, when the U.S. economy was described as "booming." What purpose did these layoffs serve beyond cost savings for the quarter or year-end report? What message did these layoffs send to the remaining workers? When businesses downsize or lay off workers, they are forever forfeiting that human capital that causes the company to be productive.

I'm not suggesting that businesses should ignore current financial or market conditions; however, if the purpose of business is "to get and keep customers," it is hard to imagine that a layoff of 144,000 workers would serve that purpose. Why were those 144,000 workers hired in the first place?

The Porsche Difference

Porsche has been an independent automobile manufacturer since the introduction of its first sports car, the Porsche 356, in 1948. The 356 was a light metal roadster based primarily on Volkswagen parts. By 1958, Porsche had built a total of 25,000 automobiles at their only facility in Gmund, Austria.

Porsche has embraced the notions that "money alone is not the mother of invention," and "Porsche must continue to grow. Not as much as possible, but as much as necessary." Porsche feels very much at home in its role of David in a world of Goliaths.

Today, Porsche builds about 55,000 cars each year and delights in telling the world that 70 percent of all the Porsches ever built are still being driven. The people at Porsche believe they enjoy customer loyalty because they have been loyal to the work they have chosen. A visit to Porsche's Website (*www.us.porsche.com*) discloses its commitment to ever improving the sports cars it builds. Its constancy of purpose is unchanged from its earliest days in the late 1940s.

Most companies use their earnings report to tout their profit projections for the next quarter or year-end report or to point out the temporary nature of any lack of profit. Every year, Porsche's annual report to Wall Street consistently declares, "We have always made a profit and we will continue to do so." Porsche feels that any projections of specific profit would make the financial projection a priority rather than its true priority: the production of great cars. This total focus on building the best sports cars can be seen in every aspect of Porsche's corporate culture.

Corporate Culture

Corporate culture always reflects the true priorities of a company. Some companies such as Porsche, Domino's, and 3M have a tradition of innovation, technical superiority, or excellence. These cultures drive employees to give their best every day in the pursuit of the company's mission. These cultures attract customers and investors who share in the company's mission.

When a company declares its purpose is profit, and jobs are a means or incentive to accomplish that purpose, the corporate culture reflects the mission. For example, some companies have laid off substantial amounts of their workforce shortly after announcing record earnings. The message to their workforces is clear, and a culture develops that supports the company's purpose. It is a culture that recognizes the temporary nature of its employment and an underlying fear of job loss.

Every business has its own unique culture. Most business organizations don't consciously try to create a certain culture. The culture of an organization typically evolves based on the values of the top management or the founders of an organization. As in every other endeavor, culture evolves more from behavior and the examples leadership provides than from what leadership says.

Business leaders who embrace a constancy of purpose of truly wanting their workers to feel fulfilled and happy demonstrate their desire and belief. They are interested in the members of their workforce as individuals with concern for them inside and outside the workplace and help establish a culture that reflects that interest. This culture manifests itself in every aspect of how employees relate to each other and, most importantly, to their customers.

When employees are threatened by ambiguity of their purpose and the value of short-term versus long-term goals, they telegraph their feelings to each other and to customers. What results is a corporate culture that recognizes that only one stakeholder really matters.

Organizational Loyalty

Frederick Reichheld, author of *The Loyalty Effect: The Hidden Force Behind Growth, Profits, and Lasting Value*, claims, "On average, U.S. corporations now lose half their customers in five years, half their employees in four, and half their investors in less than one year. We seem to face a future in which the only business relationships will be opportunistic transactions between virtual strangers."

This is an enormous problem with tremendous consequences. These defection rates affect the stability of every business. Replacing customers, employees, and investors consumes enormous sums of time and money. When more resources are spent attracting new customers, new employees, or new investors, there are fewer resources left to compensate and reward the remaining stakeholders.

Loyal customers are the cornerstones for stability in a business. Loyal customers keep coming back to buy again and again. There is no cost to attract loyal customers because they are already doing business with you. They are predictable and easier to do business with than new customers. For these reasons, loyal customers produce profits where no profit existed before. Profits can be used to attract, retain, compensate, and equip more productive workers. Ultimately, loyal customers and loyal employees benefit the company and, therefore, the investor. This is the phenomenon of organizational loyalty. Organizational loyalty benefits internal and external customers, employees, investors—all stakeholders.

The credibility collapse of many American businesses, the unemployment created by downsizing, and the loss of monumental sums of potential profit can be repaired through organizational loyalty. The book you are holding is a discussion of creating customer loyalty. Focusing on customer loyalty is the first step in developing organizational loyalty. Loyal customers are the people who show up at your front door with the money every day. Loyal customers are never the problem, they are always the solution.

Organizational loyalty fairly rewards all stakeholders. As each stakeholder is rewarded, the other stakeholders should benefit as well. Unfortunately, too often companies are swayed by Wall Street's constant scrutiny and demand for favorable quarterly or even daily earnings reports. Inevitably, these demands require a company to trade short-term rewards for long-term gains. Cost-cutting, downsizing, and layoffs are the results. The short-term investor profits, but the benefits of long-term organizational loyalty are lost.

Investors should be rewarded in proportion to their contribution of capital and risk, but their reward should not be at the expense of the other stakeholders. Organizational loyalty fairly rewards the investor when the other stakeholders are fairly rewarded.

For example, health insurance is a substantial expense. On the surface, health insurance appears to benefit only employees. The cost of health insurance premiums appears to either raise the ultimate price of goods and services charged customers or decrease the return to investors.

If we examine the benefits of providing health insurance more closely, we find companies with insured workers have less absenteeism. Workers with health benefits are more likely to take preventive health measures and submit to regular checkups. Companies that provide health benefits have healthier workers. Living without health benefits can be stressful and can produce many aliments and conditions associated with stress. Companies that provide health benefits are better able to attract more qualified and productive workers and they profit from a healthier workforce. The efficiency gained from a more productive workforce ultimately benefits customers and investors. The cost of health insurance is not at the expense of the other stakeholders, it fairly rewards all stakeholders.

Mission Statement

The starting point for creating loyalty is a mission or vision statement that declares a purpose or goal that all stakeholders can subscribe to. Because loyal customers are the ones that show up with the money every day, they should be the starting point for every mission. The sequence for reward is, customer first, employee second, and company or investor third. The phenomenon of organizational loyalty protects the company or investor from only getting the crumbs. When the customer as stakeholder benefits, loyalty is created. This loyalty produces greater net revenue to benefit both employees and investors. Creating customer loyalty rewards all stakeholders.

Domino's Pizza's mission of "Exceptional people on a mission to be the best pizza delivery company in the world" is a worthwhile goal with enormous rewards for all stakeholders. Customers, employees, and investor/owners can subscribe to the mission. The continuing accomplishment of this mission fairly benefits everyone. Domino's can attract customers, employees, and investors who all profit from organizational loyalty.

Its mission statement does not repeat Peter Drucker's directive word-for-word; however, the spirit of "The purpose of every business is to get and keep customers" is evident. If you are a Domino's Pizza customer, you are dealing with the best pizza delivery company in the world. Why wouldn't you want to be a loyal customer?

Domino's further clarifies its mission with their guiding principles:
1. We demand integrity.
2. Our people come first.

3. We take great care of our customers.
4. We make "Perfect 10" pizzas every day.
5. We operate with smart hustle and positive energy.

These guiding principles reward all stakeholders. Integrity, a superior product "Perfect 10" pizza, and operating with smart hustle are advantages to everyone. Keeping people first and taking great care of customers are fundamental to organizational loyalty.

Crafting and living by a mission statement that serves all stakeholders is an important endeavor for every business. Don't think that your company's stock has to be publicly traded for you to qualify. Your auto body shop, dry cleaners, real estate office, or insurance agency will benefit from an appropriate mission statement. Even if you own the business and are the only employee, a properly crafted mission statement will clarify and fortify your daily activities.

Many times we tend to focus on what we do not have. We tell ourselves, "I don't have the kind of customers that will ever be loyal. My employees don't stick around long enough to be stakeholders. I don't have the resources to improve and grow my business. I have fierce competition and I'm lucky just to be earning a living. Where I work, they only care about what I have done for them today."

Life is always filled with obstacles and challenges, but our obstacles and challenges can be our greatest strength.

This Restaurateur Knows His Real Strength

I met Jim Patterson several years ago. Jim grew up in Louisville during the 1940s. His family was poor and they lived on the southwest side of Louisville in the housing projects that had been built by the Works Projects Administration (WPA). Similar to most government buildings of that era, the walls of his home were yellow-glazed block, which would get pretty hot during a Louisville summer.

Jim also remembers eating fish on Fridays in accordance with his family's Catholic beliefs. The smell of fish blanketed the housing complex every week. Jim does not have fond memories of the smell or the heat.

Jim worked his way through four years of college and graduated from the University of Louisville in the early 1950s. He enlisted in the

U.S. Air Force and was stationed in a remote area. So remote that he was able to literally save all of his Air Force pay. He emerged from the Air Force with an education, $20,000, and a desire to make it big.

As soon as he returned to Louisville, Jim put an advertisement in the Louisville newspaper: "Ex-serviceman with $20,000 looking for business opportunity or partner." Jim got a ton of responses, most of them crazy schemes. He took an interest in one response and within just a few weeks he was the proud owner and franchisee of a Jerry's Restaurant on the south end of what is now Dixie Highway. Unfortunately, Dixie Highway was not a highway yet and road construction over the next several months nearly put him out of business. Jim still remembers keeping the restaurant immaculately clean when he only had a few construction workers as patrons. Eventually, the road was completed and Jim's business began to prosper. He did so well he was able to buy several more Jerry's Restaurants throughout Kentucky.

Jim was an accomplished restaurateur and businessman when he attended the National Restaurant Association meeting in San Antonio, Texas, in the mid-1960s. Jim and a few of his friends went out for dinner one night during the convention. They voted on where to dine and Jim lost the vote, so they chose a local fish house. Jim's friends assured him that this fish house was different. "This fish taste like white meat of chicken," they said. Jim was so impressed with his dinner that night that he returned to the fish house twice more during the convention.

He returned to Louisville enthusiastic about the new taste of fish he had discovered. Jim wanted the rest of the world to experience his discovery and founded Long John Silver's Seafood Shop. The concept was a hit and very quickly franchises for Jim's new restaurant began springing up all over the country. Jim later sold his interest in Long John Silver's and went on to other ventures where he enjoyed similar success.

I asked Jim, "To what do you attribute your success?" He told me, "Luck, hard work, and most of all, where I came from. I was so poor for so long. I know how to be poor. I don't like it, but I know how to be poor. For every risk I have ever taken I have been confident that if I lost everything, I could still go back to being poor. I know guys who have done well but came from money. Those guys are paralyzed when it comes to making big decisions. They are always afraid they're going to loose what they've got. Starting with nothing is the best thing that ever happened to me. There are so many people that worry they will lose their job or their business will go into a slump. I worry about those things too, but I know the loss of one thing always liberates me to find the next thing."

This book is about creating loyal customers. There are five principles that, when employed, will earn customer loyalty. Sometimes you can employ all five principles and you may still lose a customer. You may do everything right, but the outcome is not what you were hoping for. Does this mean the five principles don't work? Does this mean the five principles are a sham, a fraud? Stand back and look again. The perfection lies in your viewpoint. Your biggest losses may be your biggest learning experience. Your biggest weakness may be your biggest strength. Jim Patterson started his life thinking he had a handicap because he came from a poor family. It was not until later in life that he learned his supposed handicap was one of his greatest assets.

You may feel that you are starting with a handicap. You may feel the competition is so far ahead of you that you don't have a chance to catch up. By creating customer loyalty you can level the playing field. Loyal customers are the answer whether you own the business or you're an employee. People do business with people. When you use your unique skills, personality, and attributes to express a genuine interest in others, you have started on the path to creating loyal customers.

A Perfect World

What are your thoughts about perfection? I think perfection has to do with viewpoint or, better yet, your point of view. Think about a piece of cloth or a magnificent painting. Think about the Mona Lisa or some other great painting. Standing back from the Mona Lisa, the painting looks perfect. Artists and critics from around the world have proclaimed the beauty and perfection of the Mona Lisa. The use of color and form in this painting are considered to be examples of perfection in art.

Think about a piece of cloth. Looking at the cloth in your hands, it looks perfect. The color is uniform. As you look closer, you can see the weave of the cloth. The weave looks uniform. Each stitch is perfectly square. Or is it?

If you get close enough to the Mona Lisa or a piece of cloth, your viewpoint changes. If you use a magnifying glass or a microscope, your view changes even more. The perfection of the Mona Lisa begins to change. We can see areas where Leonardo da Vinci's brush strokes blurred lines or merged colors. If we get close enough, we can see that the Mona Lisa is anything but perfect.

It is the same with a piece of cloth. The closer we examine the cloth, the easier it is to see the imperfections. Each square of the weave is not exact. Tiny fibers are shooting in every direction. The perfection was a hoax. As soon as we get close enough, we see nothing but imperfection.

This is also true of life. The human condition is such that we tend to examine everything as if we were using a magnifying glass or a microscope. It is easy for all of us to see all the imperfections of life. We question natural disasters and premature death. We question why bad things happen to good people. We question why some people seem so incredibly successful while others who work just as hard barely get by. Maybe we see the imperfection because we are looking too close.

Remember the definition of success? "Success is making progress toward a worthwhile goal." As you move forward in your quest for loyal customers that will buy from you again and again and be delighted to tell others about your excellent goods and services, view your mistakes from a distance and view your successes up close.

There are no accidents in life. Everything that happens in this world happens for good reason. If a scientist examines an automobile crash site, she can account for every cause and effect that culminated in the crash. The weight, speed, and direction of the automobile in relation to the actions of the driver produce a result defined by physics that can only be a crash. It wasn't an accident to the universe. The only thing that could happen was the crash. The crash was an accident in terms of the driver's intent, but the universe understands that, based on the conditions, the crash was inevitable. Nothing else besides a crash could happen.

The perfection of our world is based in the nature of cause and effect. No cause occurs without an effect. This perfection exists in our every endeavor. We may not be able to account for and trace the result, or effect, of our every activity but our universe recognizes our every effort. The butterfly effect taught in rudimentary physics classes tells the story of a butterfly in Africa. When the butterfly moves its wings, it sets the surrounding air in motion. Even this minuscule effect has some impact on America, thousands of miles away. While we may not be able to feel the effect of this movement, it is still there.

The lesson of the butterfly teaches that every cause has an effect. The size and power of the cause determines the effect. A very small cause will have a very small effect, but no matter how small, there will be an effect. No cause goes with out effect. In our lives no effort goes without reward. Sometimes our efforts may not be noticed and we may never be able to account for them, but they still have effect. You and I cannot put forth effort in creating customer loyalty and not have an effect. However, like all other human endeavors, our commitment, passion, and persistence will determine our results. Our effectiveness is a function of our effort: It begins and ends with a belief in our customers and ourselves.

Spread the Word

Business is a fickle master. Whether we own our own business, work for someone else, or lead a major corporation, we can benefit from customer loyalty. Loyal customers are the only source of profit, so creating loyalty is a worthwhile goal for us as well as our customers. When we create loyalty, we create profits to add to our prosperity and growth and we better serve our customers. Creating loyalty is a winning proposition for all parties concerned.

The best thing you can do for yourself and for all the people you know is to become successful. When you are successful, you can help others attain their dreams. The more people you can help attain their desires, the more likely you are to attain your own.

Many people delude themselves about success and their prospects for success in business. They believe success is a function of luck or that it just happens for some people. They claim that the right place or the right time is the formula for success. But better than luck is the power of cause and effect. Cause and effect are working on your behalf all the time.

My most esteemed reader, I encourage you to share the message of customer loyalty. The value and benefits of customer loyalty are available for all. When you share your experience, you will be helping your family, neighbors, and business associates. The principles that create loyalty are truths, so they will work for others just as they work for you. How you apply your unique personality and skills to exercise the principles are singular: You are the only sole who can create loyalty exactly like you do. However, your lesson and example can have a huge impact on those around you. Creating loyalty is a choice. When you base your daily activities on the five principles, you are making a choice. You are making a choice to end forever your dependence on chasing new customers. You are making a choice to know, understand, help, and lead your customers. You are making a choice to serve your most important asset. You are making a choice to recognize *Why Customers Come Back!*

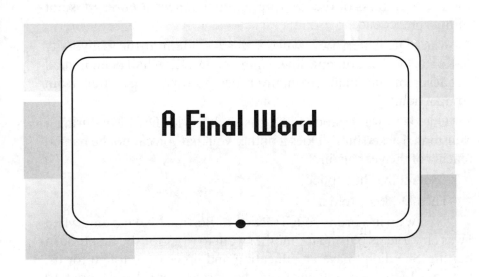

A Final Word

I recently read *Pay it Forward,* a novel by Catherine Ryan Hyde that was released in January 2000. *Pay it Forward* is a book, but it's also an idea. It's an action plan within a work of fiction from which a real-life social movement has emerged.

The movement created a Website (*www.payitforwardfoundation.org*) that tells the story. In the book, Trevor, the 12-year-old hero of *Pay It Forward*, thinks of quite an idea. He describes it to his mother and teacher this way: "You see, I do something real good for three people. And then when they ask how they can pay it back, I say they have to Pay It Forward. To three more people. Each. So nine people get helped. Then those people have to do twenty-seven." He turned on the calculator, punched in a few numbers. "Then it sort of spreads out, see. To eighty-one. Then two hundred forty-three. Then seven hundred twenty-nine. Then two thousand, one hundred eighty-seven. See how big it gets?"

The soundness of the idea presented in *Paying it Forward* is not without precedence.

I met Dr. Albert Levy when I was a student at the University of Kentucky. The students loved him and Dr. Levy had been named "Teacher of the Year" so many times he was disqualified from competition.

One day I was stranded in a bus shelter with Dr. Levy during a rainstorm. I asked him, "Does it bother you that you cannot be named teacher of the year again?"

"Not really," he replied.

Then Dr. Levy told me:

"I grew up in a pretty rough section of Boston. My Dad died when I was only 9 years old and my mother went to work for the first time in her life. She didn't have an education and times were tough for us. One day I stole a candy bar from the corner store. I was about 10 years old at the time. The fellow who owned the store was Mr. Francesconi. Mr. Francesconi saw me steal the candy bar and he stops me as soon as I step outside the door. He says, 'Albert what the hell is the matter with you. You want me to tell your mother about this?' Long story short, Mr. Francesconi tells me I've got to sweep the floor for him to make up for stealing. So I'm sweeping the floor. When I finish, he tells me to come back tomorrow, he has some other things for me to do. I go back every day after school for a week. Finally I tell him, 'Mr. Francesconi, it was just a candy bar and I've been working here for a week.' He tells me, 'I've wrapped up some pork chops for you behind the meat counter. Take the chops and a bag of potatoes home to your mother and be back here after school on Monday.' I worked for that man till I graduated from high school. He made sure we always had food on our table and sometimes I even had a couple of bucks in my pocket.

"Just before I graduated from high school Mr. Francesconi tells me, 'Albert, you can't work here the rest of your life. What are you going to do with yourself?' I told him, 'College is for rich kids and I don't have any money.' Mr. Francesconi tells me, 'If you want to go to college, I'll pay for it … but I'm not paying unless you make good grades.'"

Dr. Levy continued the story:

"Mr. Francesconi paid my way through Boston College. He paid for my tuition, books, fees. This guy paid for everything. He attended my graduation. I think he was as proud as my mother. At graduation Mr. Francesconi says to me, 'What's next, Albert?' I tell him I want to go to graduate school to get a doctorate degree. He tells me, 'You can put it on my bill.' Mr. Francesconi paid my way through graduate school. Actually, he died before I got my doctorate but in his will he left enough money so I could finish school."

Doctor Levy looked me square in the eye and said:

"He was my hero. The kids today think Superman or some baseball player is their hero. Mr. Francesconi was my hero. Mr. Francesconi taught me, you do what you can to make the world a better place. I can not repay Mr. Francesconi, but as a teacher I can make the world a better place. I owe it to everyone that ever helped me to help someone else. If the students elect me 'Teacher of the Year,' that's great, but that is not what I am about. It's more important that I know I do my best teaching every day."

In *Why Customers Come Back*, I have shared my experiences and the experiences of many others to whom I am grateful. I humbly believe that this information can have a dramatic impact on your success. But the impact from developing and using the activities that support the five principles that create customer loyalty will benefit more than just you and I. Customer loyalty also affects our businesses, customers, investors, and the communities where we do business. As business, commerce, and industry prosper, our entire society benefits. I encourage you to share the story of customer loyalty with your family, friends, and business associates. Together, through prosperity, we can make the world a better place.

Bibliography

Bettger, Frank. *How I Raised Myself From Failure to Success in Selling.* New York: Fireside, 1992.

Carnegie, Dale. *How To Win Friends and Influence People.* New York: Simon and Schuster, 1964.

Charles-Roux, Edmonde. *Chanel: Her Life, Her World, and the Woman Behind the Legend She Herself Created.* New York: Knopf, 1975.

Chopra, Deepak. *The Seven Spiritual Laws of Success.* San Rafael, Calif.: Amber-Allen Publishing and New World Library, 1994.

Cohen, Ben. *Ben & Jerry's Double Dip: Lead with Your Values and Make Money Too.* New York: Simon and Schuster, 1997.

Covey, Stephen R. *The 7 Habits of Highly Effective People.* New York: Simon and Schuster, 1989.

Crainer, Stuart. *The 75 Greatest Management Decisions Ever Made.* New York: Amacon, 1999.

Demming, W. Edwards. *Out of the Crisis.* Boston: MIT Press, 2000.

Drucker, Peter F. *The Essential Drucker.* New York: Harper Collins, 2001.

Freemantle, David. *What Customers Like About You*. London: Nicholas Brealey Publishing, 1998.

Gerstner, Louis V. Jr. *Who Says Elephants Can't Dance*. New York: Harper Business, 2002.

Gitomer, Jeffrey. *Customer Satisfaction is Worthless Customer Loyalty is Priceless: How to Make Customers Love You, Keep Them Coming Back and Tell Everyone They Know*. Bard Press, 1998.

Griffin, Jill. *Customer Loyalty: How to Earn It and How to Keep It*. New York: Jossey Bass, 1997.

Hall, Stacy and Jan Brogniez. *Attracting Perfect Customers: The Power of Strategic Synchronicity*. San Francisco: Berrett Koehler Publishers Inc., 2001.

Heskett, James L., W. Earl Sasser, and Lenonard A. Schlesinger. *The Service Profit Chain*. New York: Free Press 1997.

Lager, Fred "Chico," and Jerry Greenfield. *Ben & Jerry's: The Inside Scoop: How Two Real Guys Built a Business with a Social Conscience and a Sense of Humor*. New York: Crown Publishing, 1995.

Longaberger, Dave. *Longaberger: an American success story*. New York: Harper Business, 2001.

Lydon, Michael. *Ray Charles: man and music*. New York: Riverhead, 1998.

MacKay, Harvey. *Pushing The Envelope*. New York: Ballentine Books, 1999.

McMath, Robert. *What Were They Thinking*. New York: Times Business, 1998.

Peters, Tom. *The Circle of Innovation*. New York: Vintage Books, 1999.

Reichheld, Frederick F. *Loyalty Rules*. Boston: Harvard Business School Press, 2001.

Reichheld, Frederick F. *The Loyalty Effect: The Hidden Force Behind Business Growth*. Boston: Harvard Business School Press, 1996.

Sewell, David and Paul B. Brown. *Customers for Life.* New York: Simon and Schuster, 1998.

Silverman, George. *The Secrets of Word of Mouth Marketing.* New York: Amacon, 2001.

Spector, Robert. *Amazon.com: Get Big Fast.* New York: Harper Collins, 2002.

Tracy, Brian. *The 100 Absolutely Unbreakable Laws of Business Success.* San Francisco: Barrett Koehler Publishers Inc., 2000.

Trout, Jack. *The Power of Simplicity.* New York: McGaw Hill, 1999.

Additional Sources

www.cessna.com Cessna Aircraft

www.chicos.com Chico's

www.dominos.com Domino's Pizza

www.ford.com Ford Motor Company

www.gm.com General Motors

www.grainger.com W.W. Grainger Company

www.opi-inc.com Malden Mills

www.porsche.com Porsche

www.thckk.org Belknap Hardware

www.thetech.org Nolan Bushnell

www.toyota.com Toyota Motors

www.worldclasscatamarans.com World Class Catamarans

www.zippo.com Zippo

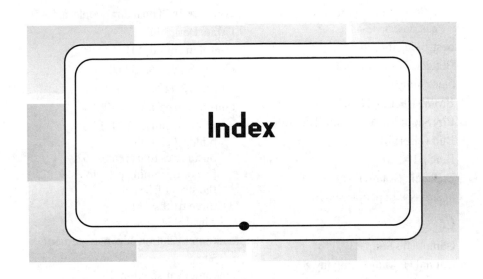

Index

About the Author

Manzie R. Lawfer is president of Loyalty Now, a consulting firm, and an expert on customer buying habits and shopping experiences. He has interviewed hundreds of business owners, captains of industry and everyday consumers. His research and studies have included a substantial sample of large corporations and small businesses.

Lawfer frequently speaks to groups but doesn't enter the room with a marching band, drop balloons from the ceiling, or offer fiery motivational speeches. By his own admission, Lawfer really only does one thing: He shows businesses and professionals how to get their customers to come back to buy again and again.

Lawfer has four sons. He and his wife, JoyAnn, live near his parents in Naples, Florida, where he skippers his 26-foot power catamaran Purrrogative.

Manzie Lawfer can be contacted through his company's Website, *www.loyaltynow.com*.